IDIOT'S GUIDES.
AS EASY AS IT GETS!

Paleo Slow Cooking

by Molly Pearl

Λ

This book would not have been written without the ceaseless support, encouragement, elbow grease, and advice of my husband, Jason. You are my coauthor, my rock, and I appreciate you every day.

ALPHA BOOKS

Published by Penguin Group (USA) Inc.

Penguin Group (USA) Inc., 375 Hudson Street, New York, New York 10014, USA • Penguin Group (Canada), 90 Eglinton Avenue East, Suite 700, Toronto, Ontario M4P 2Y3, Canada (a division of Pearson Penguin Canada Inc.) • Penguin Books Ltd., 80 Strand, London WC2R 0RL, England • Penguin Ireland, 25 St. Stephen's Green, Dublin 2, Ireland (a division of Penguin Books Ltd.) • Penguin Group (Australia), 250 Camberwell Road, Camberwell, Victoria 3124, Australia (a division of Pearson Australia Group Pty. Ltd.) • Penguin Books India Pvt. Ltd., 11 Community Centre, Panchsheel Park, New Delhi—110 017, India • Penguin Group (NZ), 67 Apollo Drive, Rosedale, North Shore, Auckland 1311, New Zealand (a division of Pearson New Zealand Ltd.) • Penguin Books (South Africa) (Pty.) Ltd., 24 Sturdee Avenue, Rosebank, Johannesburg 2196, South Africa • Penguin Books Ltd., Registered Offices: 80 Strand, London WC2R 0RL, England

International Standard Book Number: 978-1-61564-726-2
Library of Congress Catalog Card Number: Available upon request

16 15 14   8 7 6 5 4 3 2 1

Interpretation of the printing code: The rightmost number of the first series of numbers is the year of the book's printing; the rightmost number of the second series of numbers is the number of the book's printing. For example, a printing code of 14-1 shows that the first printing occurred in 2014.

Note: This publication contains the opinions and ideas of its author. It is intended to provide helpful and informative material on the subject matter covered. It is sold with the understanding that the author and publisher are not engaged in rendering professional services in the book. If the reader requires personal assistance or advice, a competent professional should be consulted. The author and publisher specifically disclaim any responsibility for any liability, loss, or risk, personal or otherwise, which is incurred as a consequence, directly or indirectly, of the use and application of any of the contents of this book.

Most Alpha books are available at special quantity discounts for bulk purchases for sales promotions, premiums, fundraising, or educational use. Special books, or book excerpts, can also be created to fit specific needs. For details, write: Special Markets, Alpha Books, 375 Hudson Street, New York, NY 10014.

Trademarks: All terms mentioned in this book that are known to be or are suspected of being trademarks or service marks have been appropriately capitalized. Alpha Books and Penguin Group (USA) Inc. cannot attest to the accuracy of this information. Use of a term in this book should not be regarded as affecting the validity of any trademark or service mark.

12/14 54986285

Publisher: *Mike Sanders*
Executive Managing Editor: *Billy Fields*
Senior Acquisitions Editor: *Brook Farling*
Development Editorial Supervisor: *Christy Wagner*
Design Supervisor: *William Thomas*

Production Editor: *Jana M. Stefanciosa*
Indexer: *Johnna VanHoose Dinse*
Layout: *Ayanna Lacey*
Proofreader: *Sara Smith*

Contents

Introduction

For as long as civilization has existed, people have hunted and gathered food. Today, people still "gather," in a sense, by shopping for food at grocery stores or farmers' markets. Eating Paleo doesn't mean you have to start hunting your own meat and foraging for greens. It does mean you'll probably eat more fresh vegetables and fruits than ever before. You also might pay more attention to the food you eat—where it was grown and how it was raised, handled, or processed.

As with any diet change, going Paleo can be challenging at times, especially when you first transition to the diet. Finding ingredients and taking time to prepare foods from scratch can be intimidating, especially if you're not all that confident in your cooking skills. Using a slow cooker and finding recipes that you like is key to success as you begin. This handy appliance does much of the work for you. You just have to prepare the ingredients, put them all in the slow cooker, and go about your day as this helpful kitchen aid cooks your dishes to perfection.

The collection of Paleo recipes in this book is designed to invite you into this new lifestyle, or offer some fresh, easy ideas for more experienced Paleo eaters. Perhaps it will challenge you to try a few new foods and become more familiar with alternative ingredients. Whatever the case, these tasty options will help keep you happily fed as you follow your own Paleo journey.

Acknowledgments

Credit is due to so many who helped shape and refine this collection of recipes. Thanks to my family, who taught me how to cook, and who instilled a deep-seated appreciation for food and the conversations a great meal can inspire. Thanks to Jason Glaspey and the entire Paleo Plan team for giving me the first opportunity to create Paleo recipes. Thanks to Brook, Christy, Bill, and everyone at Alpha Books for making my words and pictures look good and for taking a chance on a new author. Special thanks to Laurie, Tiffany and McKenzie, Sarah, Louise, Rhea, Erica and Bhargov, Erica and Alex, Casey and Allyson, Josh and Amber, Hilary, Heather, Holly and Jason, Amy, John and Kay, Anna, Elizabeth, Mike, Jesse, Kathy, and all those who loaned extra slow cookers and other equipment, helped find the right words, and tested recipes.

Chapter 1

Cooking Paleo

Welcome to the Paleo way of eating!—and to slow cooker cooking, if you haven't yet taken full advantage of this handy kitchen helper. In this chapter, you learn about eating Paleo, take a look at some of the diet's staple ingredients, and discover helpful shopping tips to get you off to a successful start.

What Is the Paleo Way of Eating?

Eating the Paleo way means, you eat as close to the natural source as possible, eliminating the modifiers, sugars, and chemicals often added to processed foods and meats. It is a diet rich in organic vegetables, fruits, nuts, and seeds as well as naturally raised meats and seafood. Because of the nature of this diet, most strict followers find themselves in the kitchen quite often. A slow cooker is the perfect tool to help ease the burden of preparing so many meals at home.

There's a rich reward for followers of the diet, however. Many have found that eating Paleo helps reduce inflammation throughout the body as well as increases energy and performance levels. It also can help you lose weight.

What Can I Eat?

This may be the most important question to ask when you start eating Paleo. These foods are largely considered acceptable: vegetables (except those on the following "What Should I Avoid?" list); fruits; meats; eggs; fish and shellfish; nuts and seeds (except peanuts, which are actually legumes); fats such as coconut, olive or avocado oil, tallow, or lard; herbal teas; raw honey; grade B maple syrup; dried and fresh herbs and spices; and sea or kosher salt.

Coffee, green and black teas, chocolate, and alcohol can also be consumed in moderation. Organic, pasture-raised, antibiotic- and hormone-free foods also are highly recommended if you can find them.

What Should I Avoid?

In general, stay away from all highly processed foods, refined sugars, artificial sweeteners, added preservatives, fats and oils not listed in the "What Can I Eat?" list, as well as factory-farmed meat, seafood, and eggs. Also avoid grains (including corn, rice, and wheat), dairy products, beans and legumes, potatoes, sugar, soda, and iodized salt.

A few Paleo ingredients are controversial, including raw dairy, grass-fed butter, agave, fresh peas, tapioca, and Brazil nuts. These ingredients have been eliminated from the recipes in this book, but you can feel free to include them as substitutions if you'd like.

Salt is a controversial ingredient in the Paleo way of eating. Some recommend you cut it out completely, while others say it's fine. In either case, it's important to replace any iodized salt in your kitchen with sea salt or kosher salt. Sea salt can be a bit coarser than kosher salt, but you can use either in these recipes. Because of the high salt content of processed foods, it might be helpful to increase the amount of sea or kosher salt you use as you transition your taste buds to the flavor and tastes of your new diet. Just be sure to use an amount that tastes good while still maintaining standards set by your medical provider.

Paleo Tips and Tricks

While the rewards are great, eating Paleo can be more expensive and labor intensive. Eliminating any of your favorite foods or getting used to unfamiliar ingredients can also be somewhat daunting. It's important to know these things up front, so you don't get discouraged later. To help you succeed at eating Paleo, here are a few tips and tricks.

Eliminate Temptation

If you're just beginning the Paleo way, it's best to get rid of anything that isn't on the list of allowable foods. You might think it's okay to keep that bag of corn chips in the house "for company," but what's going to stop you from devouring it in a late-night flurry of corn-chip munchies? If it isn't around, you won't even be tempted to eat it. Soon enough, new habits will form and you won't even miss the old temptations.

Snack, Snack, Snack

Paleo snacks are your best friends. If you aren't used to eating Paleo, you might not consume enough calories through primary meals alone. Therefore, it's important to keep your body energized by eating smaller snacks more frequently while you figure out just what your body needs. This also helps curb temptation. If you aren't hungry, you probably won't eat that slice of pizza.

Make Friends with Fat

The Paleo way of eating does not eliminate fat. In fact, *good* fats, in moderate amounts, can help keep you satiated without the extra carbs. Look for foods high in omega-3 fatty acids such as wild-caught salmon, grass-fed beef, avocados, or coconut.

Watch Your Carbs

If your primary goal is to lose weight with this diet, you might find more success by limiting your carbohydrate intake, including raw honey, maple syrup, sweet potatoes, squash, and fruit. This can vary from person to person, so find what works for you.

Season with Spices

When you're cooking from scratch and watching your salt intake, spices are essential. Spices add flavor, warmth, and depth to your base ingredients. Learn a few basic spice blends, and use them often. Or look for sugar-free spice blends like a simple curry, Italian seasoning, or poultry rub. Spices can make a basic meal exceptional.

Find Substitutions

Think you can't live without cheese? Try using sliced olives on egg scrambles or chiles for a bit of saltiness without the dairy. Spaghetti squash or zucchini ribbons easily stand in as Paleo-friendly pasta replacements. Steamed or roasted cauliflower pulsed in a food processor mimics rice. Use coconut cream as a frosting or fruit dip, or add a squeeze of lime to make a yogurt or sour cream substitute.

Learn to Love Leftovers

Cooking from raw ingredients takes time with all the washing, trimming, chopping, cooking, portioning, and storing. This is where a slow cooker really shines. You can cook huge batches and graze on leftovers all week. Or freeze individual portions and make mix-and-match meals with frozen leftovers from previous weeks. It's also easy to cook larger roasts or braises and use the main protein for other meals. For example, you could make pulled pork one night and use the leftovers as the protein in a frittata the next morning and a bit with salsa and lettuce as a wrap for lunch.

Plan for Your Week

If you don't plan to eat Paleo, you won't. It isn't always easy to swing by a restaurant and get a Paleo-friendly meal when you're tired and not in the mood to cook. So take a few minutes at the start of each week to sit down and plan out your week's meals ahead of time. You'll be more efficient at the grocery store and can rest assured that all your Paleo snack needs will be met. Then, as your week gets busy, you already know what you need to prepare for your next meal.

The amount of fat your body can handle depends on many factors. With your medical provider or nutritionist, determine what amount of fat best suits your health and diet goals.

Smart Paleo Shopping

It can take some time to get used to shopping for the Paleo way of eating, especially if you didn't do a lot of shopping for fresh ingredients before. Some ingredients might be unfamiliar to you, too. Rest assured, you'll soon find your stride and know exactly what store carries bulk almond flour and coconut aminos.

You can find most of the ingredients you'll need at a natural foods store or a larger grocer with a bulk foods section. However, with the increasing popularity of the Paleo and gluten-free ways of eating, many more grocery stores are carrying once-hard-to-find items. If you live in a remote area with limited grocery options, you can order many dry goods online in bulk.

Many processed convenience foods are not part of the Paleo way of eating—especially those with added modifiers, stabilizers, chemicals, or preservatives such as maltodextrin, propylene glycol, MSG, polysorbate 60, stearic acid, and lecithin. But you can still make Paleo eating convenient. Look for mixes of onions, celery, and carrots; butternut squash cubes; and broccoli or cauliflower florets. You also can use frozen vegetables. In addition, ask your butcher about any fresh meats that are already trimmed into the exact cut you need. Just watch out for any marinades or brines that could contain sugar.

Shop Local

Whenever possible, shop local to feast on food grown nearby and in season. This often means you get a higher quality of nutrients because the fruit and vegetables at your local farmers' market are fresher than those that spent time sitting on a freight truck or a store shelf.

Buying local meat and produce also might be less expensive because you are buying directly from the grower instead of purchasing from a grocer that increases prices to make a profit.

Buy in Bulk

Purchasing meat in bulk quantities directly from a butcher can help in two ways. First, it allows you to get prime cuts at a cheaper price by buying a quarter or half of an animal. (It will be processed and wrapped for you.) Second, it allows you to become familiar with the livestock-raising practices of the farmer producing the meat.

Read Labels

Try to buy items that don't need ingredient labels, such as whole fruits and vegetables or fresh cuts of meat. Often, the more processed a food is, the more difficult it is to pronounce the ingredients listed on the label.

Chapter 2

Slow Cooker Fundamentals

The best part of a slow cooker is that this indispensable little appliance is effortless to learn how to use. With a little planning and prep work, you can have a warm meal waiting for you when you return after a long day of work. It's nearly impossible to burn food in a slow cooker, so it's the perfect cooking method for a novice chef. You can set it and forget it!

Slow Cooker Use and Care

All sizes and shapes of slow cookers are available—big, small, round, oval, programmable, some with timers, some with thermometers. A ceramic crock, an electrical base with a heating element, a temperature gauge (usually with high and low options), and a lid are standard features for all slow cookers.

For this book, I've used three basic sizes of slow cookers:

Small: 2 or 3 quarts (2 to 3 liters)

Medium: 4 or 5 quarts (4 to 5 liters)

Large: 6 to 8 quarts (5.5 to 7.5 liters)

Most people don't have multiple slow cookers at home, so feel free to use whatever size you have as long as it's bigger than the final yield.

However, it's important to use a slow cooker with the largest surface area for any of the egg-based breakfasts, as well as the cakes. This way you can be sure the middle of the dish will set before the edges get too brown.

Time and Temperature Management

You can choose to cook most recipes on high or low, depending on how much time you have available. Typically, meat (aside from ground meat) is most tender if it's cooked on low for a longer period of time.

Some slow cookers have a warming setting that automatically turns on after a preset cooking time. It's very important that food not be kept for longer than 4 hours on a warming setting because it isn't hot enough to keep the food from spoiling.

To be sure meat is properly cooked, use a probe thermometer to check the internal temperature at intervals throughout cooking.

The following table offers a guide for minimum safe food temperatures.

Food	Minimum Internal Temperature
Chicken and poultry	165°F (75°C)
Pork	145°F (65°C)
Beef and bison	145°F (65°C)
Lamb	145°F (65°C)
Egg dishes	160°F (70°C)
Fish	145°F (65°C)

Slow Cooker Cleaning and Care

Always remove the crock from the electrical base before washing the crock, and never submerse the base in water. The ceramic crock is dishwasher safe, but the base is not. You can wipe off the base with a clean sponge if it gets dirty.

To keep the internal surface of the crock free from scratches, skip the heavy metal and use wooden, hard plastic, silicone, or rubber utensils instead.

In addition to your trusty slow cooker, a few other tools will help make your transition to the Paleo way of eating easier. Be sure to have a heavy-bottomed or nonstick skillet, mixing bowls, measuring cups and spoons, tongs, a rubber scraper, properly sharpened knives, a cutting board, parchment paper, and a sturdy wooden spoon. Several recipes call for use of an immersion blender. If you don't have one, you can put smaller batches into a food processor or blender instead. A small mandoline might be useful to quickly and evenly slice vegetables.

Tips for Slow Cooker Success

Slow cookers are simple to use, but some tips can improve your results. The helpful hints that follow can make slow cooker meals even easier.

Start on the Stovetop

Many of the recipes in this book begin with you sautéing ingredients in a skillet on the stovetop and transferring the browned ingredients to the slow cooker to finish. Meat and onions start to caramelize during this browning process, which adds a lot of flavor to the final meal. That's why it's also best to deglaze the skillet with some liquid and be sure all the browned bits in the pan are transferred to the slow cooker.

If this sounds like too much work, or if you don't have time, you can skip these steps and just throw everything in the slow cooker. The meat will often be paler in color, and you might want to increase the spices a bit to boost the flavor.

Use Parchment Paper Liners

Consider parchment paper one of your best friends when slow cooking. Lining a slow cooker crock with a layer of parchment paper helps protect the bottom surface of the food from the direct heat of the crock. But perhaps more importantly, it enables you to lift the cooked cake, frittata, or tortilla out of the crock in one piece.

Parchment paper is inexpensive and available at most grocery and kitchen supply stores, and it's easy to make a parchment liner. Simply layer two pieces of parchment, each several inches longer and wider than your slow cooker, in an X shape on the bottom of the crock and use your fingers to smooth the liner into the rounded edges and up the sides. There really isn't a fine art to the technique, as long as the bottom is mostly covered and the sides are taller than the top of whatever item you're cooking.

Don't confuse parchment with wax paper, however. Wax paper will burn in the slow cooker.

Cook with Extra Liquid

Slow cookers accumulate a lot of condensation during the cooking process, and the lid keeps all that liquid from evaporating. That's what makes slow cooker meat moist and delicious, but it does require more seasoning to keep flavors strong.

It's also best to vent the lid slightly with a wooden spoon when you're slow cooking cakes and cobblers. This prevents extra condensation from dripping down on the cake and making it mushy.

Know What to Cook, When

Some vegetables and ingredients withstand longer cooking times better than others. If you follow the recipes step by step, you'll automatically get it right.

If you prefer to substitute different vegetables, follow these simple guidelines: add root vegetables, squash, mushrooms, eggplant, peppers, onions, garlic, leeks, celery, cabbage, meat, and spices at the *beginning* of the cook time. These are heartier foods that stand up to longer cook times. Less hearty foods such as zucchini, broccoli, leafy greens, bean sprouts, fresh herbs, and seafood are better added later on, closer to the end of the cook time.

If you are using a slow cooker in a higher altitude, be sure to adjust your cook times. If possible, always use the high setting, and increase the cook time as needed. Plan on adding at least an extra hour.

Prep the Night Before

Don't have much time in the morning? Do the initial steps for a recipe the night before. Cover and refrigerate the crock overnight so all you have to do in the morning is place the crock in the electric base and turn it on.

Note your cook time might need to be increased 30 minutes or so when using this method.

Chapter 3

Energizing Breakfasts

Breakfast from a slow cooker? You bet! Your slow cooker allows you to make large batches of good-start breakfasts you can warm up for several days of leftovers. To make things even simpler, you can start some of the recipes in this chapter before you go to bed, so you can wake up to a warm, easy breakfast. Others are impressive meals you can easily serve to a larger group. Whatever your intention, the following recipes give you a protein-packed way to start your day.

Slightly sweet and very nutty, this hot breakfast cereal will keep you going all morning. Flaxseeds add just a bit of crunch along with a boost of good-for-you omega-3s.

Prep Time	Cook Time
15 minutes	3 or 4 hours

Yield	Serving Size
4 cups	1 cup

Each serving has:

720	43g	58g	26g
calories	carbohydrate	fat	protein

3 ripe bananas, peeled

2 cups almond flour

¾ cup almond butter

1½ cups unsweetened almond milk

¼ tsp. kosher salt

¼ tsp. pure vanilla extract

½ tsp. ground cinnamon

¼ tsp. freshly grated nutmeg

1 TB. flaxseeds

4 tsp. pure grade B maple syrup (optional)

1. In a 4- or 5-quart (4- to 5-liter) slow cooker, combine bananas, almond flour, almond butter, almond milk, kosher salt, vanilla extract, cinnamon, nutmeg, and flaxseeds with a wooden spoon to break up banana and almond butter.

2. Cover and cook on low for 3 or 4 hours.

3. Remove the lid, and stir porridge with a wooden spoon.

4. Serve warm with a drizzle of maple syrup (if using).

For a version with fewer carbs, skip the maple syrup and top with fresh berries and a swirl of coconut milk instead.

Almond Meal Porridge

Warm Paleo Granola

Crunchy and creamy, this quick, warm breakfast will fuel you all morning.

Prep Time	Cook Time
10 minutes	1 hour
Yield	Serving Size
5 cups	1 cup

Each serving has:

822	34g	72g	24g
calories	carbohydrate	fat	protein

1 (14-fl. oz.; 400ml) can full-fat coconut milk

5 TB. chia seeds

1 cup raw cashews

1 cup raw walnuts or pecans

½ cup raw sunflower seeds

½ cup goji berries

½ cup almond butter

¼ tsp. pure vanilla extract

½ cup unsweetened coconut flakes

1 cup fresh berries (optional)

1. In a 4- or 5-quart (4- to 5-liter) slow cooker, combine 1½ cups coconut milk, chia seeds, cashews, walnuts, sunflower seeds, goji berries, almond butter, and vanilla extract with a wooden spoon to break up almond butter.

2. Cover and cook on low for 1 hour.

3. Remove the lid, and stir in coconut flakes.

4. Serve warm, topped with fresh berries (if using) and a drizzle of remaining coconut milk.

Variation: For **Almond Chia Oatmeal,** replace the vanilla extract with almond extract, and replace the cashews with 1 cup slivered almonds. Top with fresh raspberries before serving.

You're not limited to the nuts called for in this recipe. Use your favorites or whatever you have on hand.

In this early morning take on the classic combination, crisp bacon, cherry tomatoes, and fresh basil team up with yams to give you a substantial start to your day.

Prep Time	Cook Time
15 minutes	2 to 2½ hours
Yield	Serving Size
4 slices	1 slice

Each serving has:

409	20g	10g	15g
calories	carbohydrate	fat	protein

¾ lb. (340g) yam, grated

8 large eggs

½ tsp. sea salt

¼ tsp. freshly ground black pepper

½ lb. (225g) bacon, diced

½ medium yellow onion, diced

1 cup baby spinach

2 cups cherry tomatoes

2 or 3 sprigs basil, chopped

1. Line a 6- to 8-quart (5.5- to 7.5-liter) slow cooker with parchment paper.

2. Add yam, and pat down lightly to cover the bottom of the crock.

3. Crack eggs into a medium bowl, add sea salt and black pepper, and whisk together. Set aside.

4. Heat a large skillet over medium heat. When hot, add bacon and cook, stirring frequently, for 3 to 5 minutes.

5. Add yellow onion, and sauté, stirring frequently, for 3 to 5 minutes or until slightly translucent. Remove from heat.

6. Add baby spinach to the skillet, and combine with bacon and onions.

7. Transfer bacon and vegetables to the slow cooker, and pour egg mixture over top.

8. Cover and cook on low for 2 to 2½ hours or until eggs are set.

9. Top with cherry tomatoes and basil, and serve.

For a peppery kick, replace the baby spinach with a handful of arugula, mustard, or radish greens.

BLT Breakfast Casserole

Mushroom, Shallot, and Tarragon Frittata

Earthy mushrooms and silky shallots blend with the distinctive taste of tarragon in this slow cooker breakfast. You also could serve it with mixed greens for a light lunch.

Prep Time	Cook Time
15 minutes	2 hours
Yield	Serving Size
4 slices	1 slice

Each serving has:

151	3g	9g	12g
calories	carbohydrate	fat	protein

8 large eggs

½ tsp. sea salt

¼ tsp. freshly ground black pepper

1 large shallot, diced

4 medium button mushrooms, sliced

¼ cup fresh tarragon, chopped

1. Line a 6- to 8-quart (5.5- to 7.5-liter) slow cooker with parchment paper.

2. Crack eggs into a medium bowl, add sea salt and black pepper, and whisk together. Set aside.

3. Spread out shallot, button mushrooms, and tarragon on the parchment paper in the bottom of the slow cooker. Pour in eggs.

4. Cover and cook on low for 2 hours or until eggs are set.

5. Using the parchment paper liner, gently remove frittata from the slow cooker. Serve warm or cold.

Variation: For an **Asparagus and Garlic Frittata,** replace the mushrooms and shallots with 3 asparagus spears, diced, and 2 cloves garlic, minced.

Tarragon has a very distinct taste. If you don't care for it, use any other fresh herb you like in this frittata. Try fresh basil, chives, or rosemary instead.

Creamy eggs float atop a spicy tomato and pepper sauce with thick slabs of beef in this traditional North African dish. Cool it down with a spoonful of coconut milk it if it's too spicy.

Prep Time	Cook Time
25 minutes	6 to 8 hours
Yield	Serving Size
8 cups	2 cups

Each serving has:

394	18g	21g	26g
calories	carbohydrate	fat	protein

1 tsp. ground cumin

1 tsp. paprika

2 tsp. sea salt

¼ tsp. freshly ground black pepper

12 oz. (340g) beef stew meat

2 TB. extra-virgin olive oil

1 medium yellow onion, diced

2 medium red bell peppers, ribs and seeds removed, and diced

2 large poblano peppers or green chiles, ribs and seeds removed, and diced

3 cloves garlic, sliced

½ tsp. crushed red pepper flakes (optional)

1 bay leaf

1 tsp. raw honey

1 (28-oz.; 800g) can plum tomatoes, with juice

4 large eggs

¼ cup fresh cilantro, chopped

1. In a medium bowl, combine cumin, paprika, sea salt, and black pepper. Add beef stew meat, and toss to evenly coat all sides in spice mixture.

2. Heat a medium skillet over medium heat. When hot, add extra-virgin olive oil and wait 30 seconds. Add seasoned beef stew meat (along with any residual spices), and cook, turning frequently, for 5 to 7 minutes or until slightly browned. Transfer beef to a 4- or 5-quart (4- to 5-liter) slow cooker.

3. Add yellow onion to the skillet, and cook, stirring occasionally, for 5 minutes.

4. Add red bell peppers, poblano peppers, and garlic, and cook, stirring frequently, for 5 minutes. Transfer onion mixture to the slow cooker.

5. Add crushed red pepper flakes (if using), bay leaf, honey, and plum tomatoes, with juice, to the slow cooker. Stir to break up tomatoes slightly and cover meat completely.

6. Cover and cook on low for 6 to 8 hours.

7. 30 minutes before mealtime, taste tomato sauce and season with additional sea salt if desired. Remove bay leaf, and break up any large tomato or meat pieces with a wooden spoon.

8. Increase temperature to high, cover, and cook for 15 minutes.

9. Meanwhile, crack each egg into a small cup. Using a spoon or ladle, hollow out 4 places in tomato sauce, and carefully slide 1 egg into each hollow. Repeat with remaining eggs.

10. Cover and cook for 15 to 25 minutes or until eggs are cooked to your liking.

11. Serve each egg hot over a hearty scoop of tomato sauce and garnished with cilantro.

Shakshuka
(Eggs Poached in Spicy Tomato Sauce)

Spanish Tortilla
with Chorizo

Packed with spicy chorizo and sweet vegetables, this early morning meal is easy to make ahead of time so you can cook once and eat throughout the week as leftovers.

Prep Time	Cook Time
15 minutes	2 to 2½ hours
Yield	Serving Size
4 slices	1 slice

Each serving has:			
367 calories	13g carbohydrate	24g fat	23g protein

1 medium sweet potato, sliced thin

8 large eggs

½ tsp. sea salt

¼ tsp. freshly ground black pepper

1 TB. extra-virgin olive oil

½ medium yellow onion, diced

1 medium green bell pepper, ribs and seeds removed, and diced

½ lb. (225g) ground chorizo

1. Line a 6- to 8-quart (5.5- to 7.5-liter) slow cooker with parchment paper.

2. Place sweet potato slices on the parchment paper, lining the bottom and sides of the slow cooker.

3. Crack eggs into a medium bowl, add sea salt and black pepper, and whisk together. Set aside.

4. Heat a large skillet over medium-high heat. When hot, add extra-virgin olive oil and wait 30 seconds. Add yellow onion and green bell pepper, and sauté, stirring frequently, for 3 to 5 minutes or until onions are slightly translucent.

5. Add chorizo, and cook, stirring occasionally, for 3 minutes.

6. Transfer vegetables and chorizo to the slow cooker, and spread in an even layer over sweet potatoes. Pour egg mixture over top.

7. Cover and cook on low for 2 to 2½ hours or until eggs are set.

8. Use the parchment liner to remove tortilla from the slow cooker, and serve warm or cold.

Chorizo is a flavorful pork sausage seasoned with different types of peppers. It's sold as a cured, hard sausage, or as an uncooked, ground sausage. This recipe calls for the latter, but you could easily use the same amount of hard chorizo, diced, as a replacement.

In this quick and easy breakfast, sweet root vegetables combine with savory rosemary and are topped with a perfectly fried egg.

	Prep Time	Cook Time
	15 minutes	3 hours
	Yield	Serving Size
	6 cups	1½ cups

Each serving has:

415	69g	12g	11g
calories	carbohydrate	fat	protein

2 TB. extra-virgin olive oil

2 medium yellow onions, diced

1 lb. (450g) yams, peeled and diced

1 lb. (450g) sweet potatoes, peeled and diced

1 lb. (450g) turnips, peeled and diced

1 tsp. sea salt

½ tsp. freshly ground black pepper

2 TB. fresh rosemary, minced

½ tsp. coconut oil

4 large eggs

1. Heat a medium skillet over medium-high heat. When hot, add extra-virgin olive oil, and wait 30 seconds. Add yellow onions, and sauté, stirring frequently, for 3 to 5 minutes or until slightly translucent. Transfer onions to a 4- or 5-quart (4- to 5-liter) slow cooker.

2. Add yams, sweet potatoes, turnips, sea salt, black pepper, and rosemary to the slow cooker, and stir with a wooden spoon to coat vegetables completely.

3. Cover and cook on high for 2 or 3 hours, on low for 3 or 4 hours, or until vegetables are tender.

4. Shortly before serving, heat a medium nonstick skillet over medium heat. When hot, add coconut oil and wait 30 seconds. Crack egg into the pan, and cook for 5 to 10 minutes, flipping over egg if you like, until egg is done to your liking. Repeat with remaining eggs.

5. Top each serving with 1 fried egg, and serve warm.

You can use any root vegetables you like in this recipe. However, turnips may be a bit too fibrous for a soft hash.

Root Vegetable Hash

Denver Stuffed Peppers

These flavor-packed bell peppers are bursting with ham and onions and topped with an egg for extra protein.

Prep Time	Cook Time
20 minutes	2 hours, 25 minutes
Yield	Serving Size
4 peppers	1 pepper

Each serving has:

289 calories	12g carbohydrate	16g fat	24g protein

4 medium green or red bell peppers

2 TB. extra-virgin olive oil

½ medium yellow onion, diced

½ tsp. freshly ground black pepper

1 lb. (450g) thick-sliced ham, diced

4 large eggs

Hot pepper sauce

1. Slice off top of each green bell pepper, and scoop out seeds, keeping the pepper "cup" intact. Place peppers hollow side up in the bottom of a 4- or 5-quart (4- to 5-liter) slow cooker.

2. Heat a medium skillet over medium-high heat. When hot, add extra-virgin olive oil and wait 30 seconds. Add yellow onion and black pepper to the skillet, and sauté, stirring frequently, for 3 to 5 minutes or until onions are slightly translucent.

3. Add ham, and cook, stirring occasionally, for 3 to 5 minutes or until meat begins to brown. Remove from heat.

4. Evenly distribute ham and onion mixture among peppers.

5. Cover and cook on low for 2 hours or until peppers begin to soften.

6. Crack an egg on the top of the ham and onion mixture inside each pepper. Cover and cook for 15 to 25 more minutes or until eggs are cooked the way you like them.

7. Top each pepper with a dash of hot pepper sauce, and serve.

If you're making a large batch of peppers so you have leftovers for the week, skip the eggs. Then, when you're ready to eat, reheat one pepper at a time, and top it with a quick pan-fried egg.

Chapter 4

Sustaining Snacks

Snacks are an essential part of the Paleo way of eating. The recipes in this chapter make larger quantities, so you can freeze smaller portions to grab later when you need a quick refuel. You also can use these recipes as nontraditional breakfast accompaniments or as side dishes. Hunting for easy Paleo appetizers? Look no further. Even non-Paleo guests will be impressed with these starting options.

No need to hunt down Paleo-friendly, unsweetened applesauce when it's this easy to make in the slow cooker. Spiced with cinnamon, cloves, and nutmeg, this slightly sweet version is far from bland.

Prep Time	Cook Time
10 minutes	4 to 6 hours

Yield	Serving Size
6 cups	1 cup

Each serving has:

112 calories	30g carbohydrate	0g fat	1g protein

3 lb. (1.5kg) apples, peeled, cored, and sliced

1 tsp. ground cinnamon

¼ tsp. ground nutmeg

¼ tsp. ground cloves

Juice of 1 medium lemon

1. In a 4- or 5-quart (4- to 5-liter) slow cooker, combine apples, cinnamon, nutmeg, cloves, and lemon juice, stirring to coat apples.

2. Cover and cook on low for 4 to 6 hours or until apples are mushy. Turn off slow cooker.

3. Using an immersion blender, break down apples into a smooth sauce.

4. Serve warm, right out of the slow cooker, or transfer to the refrigerator and serve chilled.

Use the sweetest variety of apples you can find. Honeycrisp and Fuji are excellent options, but avoid Red Delicious for all cooked apple recipes because they can turn grainy in the slow cooker. If the applesauce is still too tart, you can add a few tablespoons of raw honey to the batch.

Applesauce

Paleo Hummus

You'll never miss chickpeas again with this creamy, nutty version of this classic snack. Pungent garlic and a lemon zing spice up otherwise ordinary cauliflower. Yes, cauliflower!

Prep Time	Cook Time
20 minutes	3 or 4 hours
Yield	Serving Size
2½ cups	½ cup

	Each serving has:		
207 calories	9g carbohydrate	20g fat	3g protein

1½ lb. (680g) cauliflower florets (about 1 large head)

1 tsp. ground cumin

7 TB. extra-virgin olive oil

2 tsp. sea salt

½ cup tahini

3 or 4 medium cloves garlic, minced

Juice of 2 medium lemons

¼ tsp. freshly ground black pepper

¼ tsp. paprika

1. In a 4- or 5-quart (4- to 5-liter) slow cooker, combine cauliflower florets, cumin, 3 tablespoons extra-virgin olive oil, and sea salt, tossing with a wooden spoon to coat cauliflower completely.

2. Cover and cook on high for 3 or 4 hours or until cauliflower is tender. Transfer cauliflower to a food processor fitted with a chopping blade.

3. Add tahini, garlic, lemon juice, black pepper, paprika, and remaining 4 tablespoons extra-virgin olive oil, and blend until a smooth paste forms. Season with additional sea salt, lemon juice, or garlic as desired.

4. Transfer hummus to a serving bowl, sprinkle with a dash of additional paprika, and serve warm or cold with fresh vegetable slices.

Want more spice? Replace the paprika with cayenne. Don't like cumin? Just take it out! Or add more lemon or garlic, or even sliced black olives to make a more toothsome version. This basic recipe is easy to adjust as you like.

Fiery buffalo sauce covers these appetizing meatballs made with pork and beef. Serve them alongside crisp celery sticks for a cooling crunch.

Prep Time	Cook Time
40 minutes	3 hours
Yield	Serving Size
70 meatballs	7 meatballs

Each serving has:

288	4g	24g	16g
calories	carbohydrate	fat	protein

1 lb. (450g) ground pork

1 lb. (450g) 85 percent lean ground beef

1 large yellow onion, finely diced or minced

2 cloves garlic, minced

2 large eggs, beaten

½ cup almond flour

1 tsp. fresh thyme leaves

4 TB. extra-virgin olive oil

3 tsp. sea salt

½ tsp. freshly ground black pepper

8 TB. hot pepper sauce

2 TB. apple cider vinegar

2 tsp. raw honey

2 tsp. paprika

2 tsp. granulated garlic

Celery sticks

1. In a large bowl, combine pork, beef, yellow onion, garlic, eggs, almond flour, thyme, 1 tablespoon extra-virgin olive oil, 2 teaspoons sea salt, and black pepper.

2. Using a heaping tablespoon measure, form mixture into 70 meatballs.

3. Heat a medium nonstick skillet over medium-high heat. When hot, add 1 tablespoon extra-virgin olive oil and wait 30 seconds. Add meatballs to cover the bottom of the skillet. Cook, turning once, for 5 to 7 minutes or just until browned. Transfer browned meatballs to a 4- or 5-quart (4- to 5-liter) slow cooker, and repeat for remaining meatballs.

4. In a small bowl, whisk together remaining 2 tablespoons extra-virgin olive oil, remaining 1 teaspoon sea salt, hot pepper sauce, apple cider vinegar, honey, paprika, and granulated garlic. Add to the slow cooker.

5. Cover and cook on low for 2 or 3 hours or until meatballs reach an internal temperature of 160°F (70°C).

6. Serve meatballs warm with celery sticks.

Use whatever hot pepper sauce you like. Some have a minimal amount of questionable Paleo ingredients, but if you spend a little more, you can find some completely Paleo friendly.

Buffalo-Style Meatballs

Dolmas
(Stuffed Grape Leaves)

Aromatic cumin, coriander, cinnamon, and allspice season hearty ground lamb in this Middle Eastern recipe. Brightened with fresh lemon juice, mint, parsley, and dill, these bite-size snacks are the perfect savory treat.

Prep Time	Cook Time
30 minutes	3 to 8 hours
Yield	Serving Size
28 dolmas	4 dolmas

Each serving has:			
300 calories	3g carbohydrate	25g fat	11g protein

28 brined grape leaves

1 large white onion, coarsely chopped

2 cloves garlic

2 TB. fresh mint

2 TB. fresh parsley

2 TB. fresh dill

5 TB. extra-virgin olive oil

2 tsp. sea salt

¼ tsp. freshly ground black pepper

½ tsp. ground cumin

½ tsp. ground coriander

⅛ tsp. ground cinnamon

⅛ tsp. allspice

2 cups cauliflower florets (about ½ large head)

1 lb. (450g) ground lamb

Juice of 2 medium lemons

1. Drain grape leaves of brine, remove stems, and soak leaves in a bowl of hot water for 15 minutes or until soft.

2. Meanwhile, in a food processor fitted with a chopping blade, pulse together white onion, garlic, mint, parsley, dill, 1 tablespoon extra-virgin olive oil, sea salt, black pepper, cumin, coriander, cinnamon, and allspice for 15 seconds or until a rough paste forms.

3. Add cauliflower florets, and pulse a few more times or until cauliflower is in rice-size pieces.

4. In a large bowl, combine cauliflower mixture with ground lamb.

5. Place 1 soft grape leaf on a clean surface. Spoon 2 tablespoons ground lamb mixture in the center, tuck both ends of leaf over lamb mixture, and roll leaf into a snug packet. Place in the bottom of a 6- to 8-quart (5.5- to 7.5-liter) slow cooker, and repeat with remaining grape leaves. Add a second layer of dolmas on top of the first when the bottom of the crock is covered.

6. Drizzle dolmas with lemon juice and remaining 4 tablespoons extra-virgin olive oil.

7. Cover and cook on low for 6 to 8 hours, on high for 3 or 4 hours, or until lamb reaches an internal temperature of 160°F (70°C).

8. Serve warm or cold, with additional lemon juice as desired.

These potato snacks satisfy both your sweet and savory cravings in just a few easy steps.

Prep Time	Cook Time
5 minutes	2 or 3 hours
Yield	Serving Size
4 cups	1 cup

Each serving has:

145 calories	27g carbohydrate	4g fat	2g protein

3 lb. (1.5kg) sweet potatoes

1 TB. extra-virgin olive oil

½ tsp. sea salt

½ tsp. dried thyme

1. Using a sharp knife, slice sweet potatoes crosswise into ½-inch (1.25-centimeter) discs.

2. Add sweet potato slices, extra-virgin olive oil, sea salt, and thyme to a 4- or 5-quart (4- to 5-liter) slow cooker, and stir with a wooden spoon to completely coat sweet potatoes.

3. Cover and cook on low for 2 or 3 hours or until sweet potatoes are tender.

4. Serve warm.

These scrumptious sweet potatoes are terrific served warm as a side, or you can refrigerate them for a quick snack later.

Baked Sweet Potatoes

with Thyme

Chapter 5

Vegetable Soups, Stews, and More

Vegetables rarely are the featured ingredient in the Paleo way of eating, but the recipes in this chapter are sure to please even the most meat-loving palates. When slow cooker cooking, use shorter cook times to keep your veggies from turning to mush. Or you can use an immersion blender to make a smooth and satisfying puréed soup so you don't have to think twice about it.

Vegetable Broth

This vitamin- and mineral-rich broth is earthy and adaptable. With its root vegetable base, it's a perfect addition to any recipe.

Prep Time	Cook Time
10 minutes	8 to 24 hours
Yield	Serving Size
4 quarts (4 liters)	2 cups

Each serving has:

109 calories	18g carbohydrate	3g fat	4g protein

2 large leeks, sliced

2 cloves garlic, crushed

3 medium turnips, halved

1 medium parsnip, sliced

2 medium carrots, sliced

2 stalks celery, sliced

4 medium mushrooms (fresh or dried; any variety)

1 TB. sea salt

1 tsp. whole black peppercorns

1 bay leaf

1 tsp. dried thyme

1 tsp. dried parsley (or several fresh sprigs)

Juice of 1 medium lemon

5 qt. (4.75l) water

1. In a 6- to 8-quart (5.5- to 7.5-liter) slow cooker, combine leeks, garlic, turnips, parsnip, carrots, celery, mushrooms, sea salt, black peppercorns, bay leaf, thyme, parsley, lemon juice, and water.

2. Cover and cook on low for 8 to 24 hours.

3. Strain through a fine sieve to separate vegetables from broth. Discard vegetables.

4. Use broth immediately as a base for soups or stews, or freeze in portions for later use.

There's no need to trim or peel the vegetables for this broth, but do clean them, of course. And feel free to use whatever vegetable scraps you have on hand if what's called for here aren't among your favorites.

This beautiful magenta soup features the winning combination of sweet potatoes, coconut milk, and beets, with a hearty helping of fragrant garlic and lemon juice.

Prep Time	Cook Time
15 minutes	2 to 6 hours
Yield	Serving Size
9 cups	3 cups

Each serving has:

194 calories	35g carbohydrate	5g fat	4g protein

2 TB. coconut or olive oil

1 large yellow onion, diced

2 medium carrots, trimmed and diced

2 cloves garlic, crushed

1 medium fennel bulb, trimmed and diced

4 cups vegetable broth

2 large sweet potatoes, peeled and diced

5 medium beets, peeled and diced

1 bay leaf

½ tsp. sea salt

¼ tsp. freshly ground black pepper

Juice of 1 medium lemon

Coconut milk

1. Heat a large skillet over medium-high heat. When hot, add coconut oil and wait 30 seconds. Add yellow onion and carrots, and sauté, stirring frequently, for 3 to 5 minutes or until onions are slightly translucent.

2. Add garlic and fennel, and cook, stirring occasionally, for 3 to 5 minutes or until vegetables begin to turn golden brown. Transfer vegetables to a 4- or 5-quart (4- to 5-liter) slow cooker.

3. Pour ½ cup vegetable broth into the hot pan, and use a wooden spoon to loosen browned bits. Pour vegetable broth and browned bits into the slow cooker.

4. Add remaining 3½ cups vegetable broth, sweet potatoes, beets, bay leaf, sea salt, and black pepper to the slow cooker.

5. Cover and cook on low for 4 to 6 hours, on high for 2 or 3 hours, or until vegetables are soft.

6. Using an immersion blender, purée soup in the slow cooker.

7. Add lemon juice, and adjust sea salt to taste. Drizzle with coconut milk, and serve.

To add extra protein to this light meal, top each serving with 4 ounces (110 grams) sliced chicken breast, shredded pork, or grilled steak.

Sweet Beet Soup

Roasted Red Pepper and Tomato Soup

Flavorful fire-roasted tomatoes and red peppers blend with a savory carrot and onion base in this silky smooth soup.

Prep Time	Cook Time
15 minutes	2 to 6 hours
Yield	Serving Size
8 cups	2 cups

Each serving has:

246 calories	33g carbohydrate	8g fat	5g protein

2 TB. extra-virgin olive oil

1 large yellow onion, diced

2 cloves garlic, crushed

1 (28-oz.; 800g) can fire-roasted, crushed tomatoes, with juice

1 (12-oz.; 340g) jar roasted red peppers, drained

1 large carrot, trimmed, peeled, and sliced

4 cups vegetable broth

1 tsp. sea salt

¼ tsp. freshly ground black pepper

2 tsp. dried basil

1. Heat a medium skillet over medium-high heat. When hot, add extra-virgin olive oil and wait 30 seconds. Add yellow onion and garlic, and sauté, stirring frequently for 3 to 5 minutes or until onions are slightly translucent. Transfer vegetables to a 4- or 5-quart (4- to 5-liter) slow cooker.

2. Add tomatoes with juice, roasted red peppers, carrot, vegetable broth, sea salt, black pepper, and basil, and stir with a wooden spoon.

3. Cover and cook on low for 4 to 6 hours, on high for 2 or 3 hours, or until vegetables are soft.

4. Using an immersion blender, purée soup in the slow cooker.

5. Adjust sea salt and black pepper to taste, and serve warm or cold.

You can roast your own peppers if you'd like. For this recipe, use 2 large red bell peppers. Place the whole peppers on a metal baking sheet, and bake at 450°F (230°C) for 30 to 45 minutes or until the skins are soft. Let cool. Remove the skin, stems, and seeds before placing in the slow cooker.

Tender butternut squash and robust fennel combine with a hint of orange and fresh dill in this simple but sensational soup.

Prep Time	Cook Time
15 minutes	2 to 6 hours
Yield	Serving Size
8 cups	2 cups

Each serving has:

328	61g	9g	7g
calories	carbohydrate	fat	protein

2 TB. coconut or olive oil

1 large yellow onion, diced

2 cloves garlic, crushed

1 medium fennel bulb, trimmed and diced

4 cups vegetable broth

1 small (3-lb.; 1.5kg) butternut squash, peeled and diced

½ tsp. sea salt

¼ tsp. freshly ground black pepper

Juice of 1 large orange

½ cup fresh dill weed, chopped

1. Place a large skillet over medium-high heat. When hot, add coconut oil and wait 30 seconds. Add yellow onion, and sauté, stirring frequently, for 3 to 5 minutes or until slightly translucent.

2. Add garlic and fennel, and cook, stirring occasionally, for 3 to 5 minutes or until vegetables begin to turn golden brown. Transfer vegetables to a 4- or 5-quart (4- to 5-liter) slow cooker.

3. Pour ½ cup vegetable broth into the hot pan, and use a wooden spoon to loosen browned bits. Pour vegetable broth and browned bits into the slow cooker.

4. Add remaining 3½ cups vegetable broth, butternut squash, sea salt, and black pepper to the slow cooker.

5. Cover and cook on low for 4 to 6 hours, on high for 2 or 3 hours, or until vegetables are soft.

6. Add orange juice, and adjust sea salt to taste. Top with fresh dill, and serve.

This soup is excellent as is, but you could use an immersion blender to make a puréed version if you prefer.

Butternut Squash Soup
with Orange

Green Ginger Soup

Dark greens and warm ginger are brightened with lemon and a hint of cumin in this good-for-you soup. Serve cold for a refreshing summer lunch or warm for a wintertime boost of greens.

Prep Time	Cook Time
20 minutes	2 to 6 hours
Yield	Serving Size
6 cups	2 cups

Each serving has:

247	35g	11g	8g
calories	carbohydrate	fat	protein

2 TB. coconut or olive oil

1 large yellow onion, diced

1 large leek, white and light green parts chopped

2 cloves garlic, minced

4 cups vegetable broth

1 large sweet potato, peeled and diced

1 lb. (450g) kale or chard, stems removed and leaves chopped

1 cup fresh cilantro, chopped

3 TB. freshly peeled and grated gingerroot

1 tsp. ground cumin

1 tsp. sea salt

½ tsp. freshly ground black pepper

Juice of ½ medium lemon

1. Heat a medium skillet over medium-high heat. When hot, add coconut oil and wait 30 seconds. Add yellow onion and leek, and sauté, stirring frequently, for 3 to 5 minutes or until vegetables are slightly translucent.

2. Add garlic, and cook, stirring occasionally, for 3 to 5 minutes or until vegetables begin to turn golden brown. Transfer vegetables to a 4- or 5-quart (4- to 5-liter) slow cooker.

3. Pour ½ cup vegetable broth into the hot pan, and use a wooden spoon to loosen browned bits. Pour vegetable broth and browned bits into the slow cooker.

4. Add remaining 3½ cups vegetable broth, sweet potato, kale, cilantro, gingerroot, cumin, sea salt, and black pepper to the slow cooker.

5. Cover and cook on low for 4 to 6 hours, on high for 2 or 3 hours, or until vegetables are soft.

6. Use an immersion blender to purée soup in the slow cooker.

7. Add lemon juice and adjust sea salt to taste just before serving.

If you don't like cilantro, you can substitute the same amount of fresh parsley for a different flavor. Also, feel free to add whatever greens or fresh herbs you have on hand.

This North African stew takes its flavor from harissa, a Tunisian hot chile pepper paste that combines well with fresh cilantro and cooling mint.

	Prep Time	Cook Time
	15 minutes	2 to 6 hours
	Yield	Serving Size
	3 quarts (3 liters)	2 cups

Each serving has:

170 calories	23g carbohydrate	8g fat	3g protein

3 TB. coconut or olive oil

1 large yellow onion, diced

2 cloves garlic, crushed

1 TB. Moroccan spice blend

4 cups vegetable broth

2 medium carrots, trimmed, peeled, and sliced

1 small (3-lb.; 1.5kg) butternut squash, peeled and diced

2 medium tomatoes, diced

2 to 4 tsp. harissa (depending on your spice preference)

1 tsp. sea salt

½ tsp. freshly ground black pepper

2 medium zucchini, diced

Juice of 1 medium lemon

½ cup fresh cilantro, chopped

½ cup fresh mint, chopped

1. Heat a large skillet over medium-high heat. When hot, add coconut oil and wait 30 seconds. Add yellow onion, garlic, and Moroccan spice blend, and sauté, stirring frequently, for 3 to 5 minutes or until onions are slightly translucent. Transfer onion mixture to a 4- or 5-quart (4- to 5-liter) slow cooker.

2. Pour ½ cup vegetable broth into the hot pan, and use a wooden spoon to loosen browned bits. Pour vegetable broth and brown bits into the slow cooker.

3. Add remaining 3½ cups vegetable broth, carrots, butternut squash, tomatoes, harissa, sea salt, and black pepper to the slow cooker.

4. Cover and cook on low for 4 hours or on high for 2 hours.

5. Add zucchini and lemon juice, stir, and cook for 1 or 2 more hours or until vegetables are tender.

6. Sprinkle with fresh cilantro and mint to serve.

To make a Moroccan spice blend, combine 1 teaspoon ground cinnamon, 1 teaspoon ground cumin, ¼ teaspoon ground cloves, ¼ teaspoon ground ginger, ¼ teaspoon turmeric, and ¼ teaspoon allspice.

Moroccan Vegetable Stew
with Harissa

Braised Fennel
with Figs and Bay Leaves

Licorice-sweet fennel combines with floral figs and bay leaves to create a distinctly European-flavored dish.

Prep Time	Cook Time
10 minutes	2 or 3 hours
Yield	Serving Size
4 bulbs	1 bulb

Each serving has:

169	73g	1g	10g
calories	carbohydrate	fat	protein

3 lb. (1.5kg) fennel bulbs, trimmed and halved

2 small shallots, peeled and sliced

16 dried figs, stems removed and halved

1 cup vegetable broth

½ tsp. sea salt

¼ tsp. freshly ground black pepper

6 bay leaves

1 (2-in.; 5cm) cinnamon stick (optional)

1. Place fennel bulb halves cut side down in a 4- or 5-quart (4- to 5-liter) slow cooker.

2. Arrange shallots and figs around fennel bulbs, pour in vegetable broth, and sprinkle sea salt and black pepper over top.

3. Tuck bay leaves and cinnamon stick around fennel bulbs.

4. Cover and cook on low for 2 or 3 hours or until fennel bulbs are soft.

5. Remove bay leaves and cinnamon stick before serving.

High in vitamin C and potassium, fennel is also considered to have many medicinal properties. It's full of antioxidants as well.

In this simple vegetable dish, eggplant and zucchini are slow cooked in juicy tomatoes and seasoned with a classical French herb blend.

Prep Time	Cook Time
15 minutes	2 or 3 hours
Yield	Serving Size
4 cups	1 cup

Each serving has:			
141 calories	18g carbohydrate	8g fat	4g protein

2 TB. extra-virgin olive oil

1 large yellow onion, diced

2 cloves garlic, crushed

1 large eggplant, trimmed and diced

2 medium zucchini, cut into ½-in. (1.25cm) discs

2 medium tomatoes, diced

1 cup vegetable broth

1 tsp. herbes de Provence

2 tsp. sea salt

½ tsp. freshly ground black pepper

1. Heat a large skillet over medium-high heat. When hot, add extra-virgin olive oil and wait 30 seconds. Add yellow onion and garlic, and sauté, stirring frequently, for 3 to 5 minutes or until onions are slightly translucent. Transfer onions and garlic to a 4- or 5-quart (4- to 5-liter) slow cooker.

2. Add eggplant, zucchini, tomatoes, vegetable broth, herbes de Provence, sea salt, and black pepper to the slow cooker, and stir to combine.

3. Cover and cook on low for 2 or 3 hours or until vegetables are tender.

4. Season with additional sea salt before serving.

Rosemary, thyme, oregano, basil, marjoram, and savory are combined in the classic herbes de Provence blend. Fennel, sage, or lavender are also included in some varieties.

Ratatouille

Chapter 6

Chicken and Poultry Entrées

Few dishes are as versatile or simple to prepare as a chicken dinner. In addition, your slow cooker brings a convenience that's hard to beat for these staple Paleo dishes. Whether it's a flavorful curry, a spicy chili, or a mellow braise, the chicken, turkey, and other poultry entrées in this chapter are satisfying and delicious.

Chicken Bone Broth

This rich and soothing broth is bursting with creamy chicken flavor and a hint of aromatic fennel and rosemary.

Prep Time	Cook Time
10 minutes	8 to 24 hours

Yield	Serving Size
4 quarts (4 liters)	2 cups

Each serving has:

60 calories	0g carbohydrate	6g fat	2g protein

2 lb. (1kg) chicken bones

1 large yellow onion, quartered

2 cloves garlic, crushed

2 medium carrots, sliced

2 celery stalks, sliced

1 TB. sea salt

1 tsp. whole black peppercorns

2 bay leaves

1 tsp. rosemary

1 tsp. fennel seed

2 TB. apple cider vinegar

5 qt. (4.75l) water

1. In a 6- to 8-quart (5.5- to 7.5-liter) slow cooker, combine chicken bones, yellow onion, garlic, carrots, celery, sea salt, black peppercorns, bay leaves, rosemary, fennel seed, apple cider vinegar, and water.

2. Cover and cook on low for 8 to 24 hours.

3. Strain through a fine sieve to separate bones and vegetables from broth. Discard bones and vegetables.

4. Use broth immediately as a base for soups or stews, or freeze in portions for later use.

For easier broth making, it's helpful to keep a container of scraps in the freezer. Place bones, vegetable trimmings, or wilted greens in the container as you have them so they're ready to use when you want to make broth. If you cook frequently, you shouldn't have to buy vegetables specifically to make broth.

Browned chicken thighs provide a savory complement to sweet yams and succulent leafy greens, while jalapeños add an unexpected zip to this satisfying soup.

Prep Time	Cook Time
25 minutes	3 to 6 hours
Yield	Serving Size
4 quarts (4 liters)	2 cups

Each serving has:

257 calories	17g carbohydrate	12g fat	21g protein

1 tsp. sea salt

½ tsp. freshly ground black pepper

6 (5-oz.; 140g) boneless, skinless chicken thighs, cut into 1-in. (2.5cm) cubes

2 TB. coconut oil

1 large yellow onion, diced

2 cloves garlic, minced

1 medium carrot, peeled and chopped

1 tsp. dried thyme

½ tsp. dried oregano

4 cups chicken or vegetable broth

4 cups water

1 bay leaf

1 (2-oz.; 55g) can jalapeños, drained, seeded, and diced

1 large yam, diced

1 lb. (450g) chard, stems trimmed and leaves roughly chopped

8 green onions, white and green parts sliced

Juice of ½ large lemon

1. In a medium bowl, combine ¼ teaspoon sea salt and ¼ teaspoon freshly ground black pepper. Add chicken cubes, and toss until cubes are fully coated.

2. Heat a large skillet over medium-high heat. When hot, add coconut oil and wait 30 seconds. Add yellow onion, garlic, carrot, thyme, and oregano, and sauté, stirring frequently, for 3 to 5 minutes or until vegetables are slightly softened and onions are translucent.

3. Add chicken cubes to the skillet, and sauté, stirring frequently, for 5 minutes.

4. Remove the skillet from heat, and transfer chicken and vegetables to a 6- to 8-quart (5.5- to 7.5-liter) slow cooker.

5. Add chicken broth, water, bay leaf, jalapeños, yam, chard, and green onions to the slow cooker.

6. Cover and cook on low for 5 or 6 hours, on high for 3 or 4 hours, or until chicken is cooked through and tender.

7. Remove bay leaf, taste soup, and season with remaining sea salt and black pepper as needed.

8. Stir in fresh lemon juice, and serve hot.

To get the richest flavor out of browned chicken in your soup, add ¼ cup chicken broth to the hot skillet after transferring the contents of the pan to the slow cooker. Use a firm rubber scraper to loosen all browned bits off the bottom of the pan, and add the broth and browned bits to the slow cooker.

Chicken, Yam, and Chard Soup

Tom Kha Gai
(Thai Chicken Soup)

Fragrant lemongrass, galangal, Kaffir lime, and coriander enhance the natural sweetness of coconut in this easy Thai soup.

Prep Time	Cook Time
15 minutes	3½ to 6½ hours
Yield	Serving Size
8 cups	2 cups

Each serving has:

552	13g	41g	51g
calories	carbohydrate	fat	protein

6 cups chicken broth

1 (2-in.; 5cm) piece fresh galangal root, peeled and sliced

3 kaffir lime leaves

1 stalk fresh lemongrass, sliced

1 or 2 red Thai chiles, halved

1 TB. whole coriander seeds

1 lb. (450g) boneless, skinless chicken breasts

1 tsp. sea salt

1 lb. (450g) straw or white button mushrooms

2 (14-fl. oz.; 400ml) cans full-fat coconut milk

2 or 3 TB. high-quality fish sauce

½ cup fresh cilantro, chopped

Chile oil (optional)

1. In a 4- or 5-quart (4- to 5-liter) slow cooker, combine chicken broth, galangal root, kaffir lime leaves, lemongrass, Thai chiles, and coriander seeds.

2. Cover and cook on low for 6 hours on high for 3 hours.

3. Meanwhile, slice chicken breasts into ¼-inch (.5-centimeter) slices against the grain. Season with sea salt, and refrigerate for later use.

4. Strain soup, discarding galangal root, kaffir lime leaves, lemongrass, Thai chilies, and coriander seeds. Return broth to the slow cooker.

5. Add sliced chicken, straw mushrooms, coconut milk, and fish sauce, and stir.

6. Cover and cook for 30 minutes or until chicken is cooked through.

7. Garnish with fresh cilantro and chile oil (if using), and serve.

If you like really spicy dishes, you can increase the number of Thai chiles in this recipe. If you have trouble finding fresh galangal root, you can substitute fresh gingerroot, but the flavor will vary. And be sure to look for chile oil with an olive oil base instead of vegetable oil.

In this soup, hearty chicken thighs are slow cooked in green curry and coconut milk and topped with an assortment of bright vegetables and fresh basil.

Prep Time	Cook Time
20 minutes	3 to 6 hours
Yield	Serving Size
8 cups	2 cups

Each serving has:

437	17g	27g	44g
calories	carbohydrate	fat	protein

2 tsp. sea salt

2 TB. green curry powder or paste

1½ lb. (680g) boneless, skinless chicken thighs, cut into 2-in. (5cm) cubes

1 (14-fl. oz.; 400ml) can full-fat coconut milk

¾ lb. (340g) cauliflower florets

4 cloves garlic, minced

1 (1-in.; 2.5cm) piece fresh gingerroot, grated

¾ lb. (340g) green beans, trimmed and chopped

1 medium red bell pepper, ribs and seeds removed, and sliced

½ cup fresh basil, chopped

1. In a medium bowl, combine sea salt and green curry powder. Add chicken cubes, and toss until fully coated. Transfer chicken to a 4- or 5-quart (4- to 5-liter) slow cooker.

2. Add coconut milk, cauliflower, garlic, and gingerroot to the slow cooker, and stir with a wooden spoon.

3. Cover and cook on low for 4 hours or on high for 2 hours.

4. Add green beans and red bell pepper, cover, and cook for 1 hour or until chicken is cooked through and vegetables are tender.

5. Taste and season with additional sea salt if needed.

6. Top with fresh basil, and serve.

Add any kind of vegetables you'd like to this curry. If you opt for carrots, hearty greens, cabbage, fennel, eggplant, or root vegetables, add them at the very beginning. For more delicate vegetables like zucchini, tender greens, or diced tomatoes, wait until the end to add them.

Green Curry Chicken
with Coconut and Basil

Chicken Legs
with Garlic, Lemon, and Artichokes

A sweet and savory spice rub adds flavor to whole chicken legs that are served over a bed of wilted chard with garlic, lemon slices, artichokes, and olives.

Prep Time	Cook Time
20 minutes	3 to 6 hours
Yield	Serving Size
4 chicken legs, 4 cups vegetables	1 leg, 1 cup vegetables

Each serving has:

324 calories	12g carbohydrate	15g fat	37g protein

1 tsp. sea salt

½ tsp. freshly ground black pepper

½ tsp. paprika

½ tsp. ground coriander

½ tsp. ground ginger

¼ tsp. ground cinnamon

¼ tsp. ground cloves

2 TB. plus 1 tsp. extra-virgin olive oil

4 (6-oz.; 170g) bone-in, skin-on whole chicken legs

1 lb. (450g) Swiss chard, chopped

½ small lemon, quartered and sliced

2 cloves garlic, peeled and sliced

1 cup brined artichoke hearts, drained

½ cup green olives, pitted

¼ cup chicken stock

1. In a medium bowl, combine sea salt, black pepper, paprika, coriander, ginger, cinnamon, cloves, and 2 tablespoons extra-virgin olive oil.

2. Gently rub each chicken leg with spice-and-oil mixture under and over skin. Set aside.

3. In the bottom of a 4- or 5-quart (4- to 5-liter) slow cooker, place Swiss chard, lemon slices, garlic, artichoke hearts, and green olives.

4. Heat a medium skillet over medium-high heat. When hot, add remaining 1 teaspoon extra-virgin olive oil and wait 30 seconds. Add chicken legs to the hot pan, and cook for 1 to 3 minutes or until lightly browned. Turn over chicken, and repeat on the other side. Add chicken to the slow cooker.

5. Pour chicken stock into the hot pan, and use a wooden spoon to loosen browned bits. Pour chicken stock and browned bits over chicken in the slow cooker.

6. Cover and cook on low for 6 to 8 hours, on high for 3 or 4 hours, or until chicken reaches an internal temperature of 165°F (75°C).

7. Season to taste with sea salt, and serve.

Because of all the steam and liquid in the slow cooker, the chicken skin won't stay crisp. To get a crisper skin, you can remove the chicken legs after they come to a safe temperature and broil them on high for 2 or 3 minutes.

This easy roasted chicken dish highlights the subtle flavor of crimini mushrooms, robust kale, and herbal sage.

Prep Time	Cook Time
15 minutes	3 or 4 hours
Yield	Serving Size
1 chicken	1 chicken quarter

Each serving has:

680 calories	31g carbohydrate	25g fat	104g protein

1 lb. (450g) kale, stems removed and roughly chopped

10 medium crimini mushrooms, sliced

4 oz. (110g) shallots, diced (about 2 small shallots)

½ cup chicken stock

1 tsp. sea salt

½ tsp. freshly ground black pepper

1 TB. dried sage leaves

2 TB. extra-virgin olive oil

1 (3-lb.; 1.5kg) chicken, quartered

1. In a 6- to 8-quart (5.5- to 7.5-liter) slow cooker, place kale, crimini mushrooms, shallots, and chicken stock.

2. In a small bowl, combine sea salt, black pepper, sage, and extra-virgin olive oil.

3. Gently rub chicken quarters, both under and over the skin, with sage-and-oil mixture. Arrange chicken on top of kale and mushrooms in the slow cooker.

4. Cover and cook on high for 3 or 4 hours or until chicken reaches an internal temperature of 165°F (75°C).

5. Taste and season with additional sea salt, if desired, and remove skin before serving.

It's important to use a thermometer to check the internal temperature of the whole chicken. It's also best to cook this on high to quickly bring the meat to a food-safe temperature.

Whole Roasted Chicken
with Kale and Mushrooms

Braised Cornish Hens
with Cardamom and Garlic

Scents of cardamom and garlic combine to flavor small Cornish hens that are cooked with a splash of white wine and served over dark kale.

Prep Time	Cook Time
20 minutes	3 to 6 hours
Yield	Serving Size
2 Cornish hens	½ hen

Each serving has:			
686 calories	12g carbohydrate	46g fat	56g protein

1 tsp. sea salt

¼ tsp. freshly ground black pepper

8 cardamom pods, crushed, with hulls discarded

½ tsp. dried oregano

2 cloves garlic, minced

2 TB. plus 1 tsp. extra-virgin olive oil

2 small Cornish hens, cleaned and halved

1 cup dry white wine

1 lb. (450g) kale, stems removed and roughly chopped

1. In a medium bowl, combine sea salt, black pepper, cardamom pods, oregano, garlic, and 2 tablespoons extra-virgin olive oil.

2. Gently rub each Cornish hen half with the spice and oil mixture under and over the skin. Set aside.

3. Heat a large skillet over medium-high heat. When hot, add remaining 1 teaspoon extra-virgin olive oil and wait 30 seconds. Add 2 Cornish hen halves to the pan, and cook for 1 to 3 minutes or until lightly browned. Turn over halves, and repeat on other side. Transfer browned halves to a 6- to 8-quart (5.5- to 7.5-liter) slow cooker. Repeat with remaining halves.

4. Pour white wine into the pan, and use a wooden spoon to loosen browned bits. Pour white wine and browned bits into the slow cooker, along with kale.

5. Cover and cook on low for 6 or 7 hours, on high for 3 or 4 hours, or until poultry reaches an internal temperature of 165°F (75°C).

6. Serve warm, and remove skin if desired.

Cornish hens are often available in the frozen food section of supermarkets. If you can't find them, you can substitute a 3- or 4-pound (1.5- to 2-kilogram) chicken instead.

This lighter turkey chili packs a flavorful punch with zucchini, onions, garlic, cumin, and green chiles.

Prep Time	Cook Time
15 minutes	2½ to 6 hours
Yield	Serving Size
10 cups	2 cups

Each serving has:

398	13g	25g	31g
calories	carbohydrate	fat	protein

2 TB. extra-virgin olive oil

1 medium yellow onion, diced

1 clove garlic, minced

2 lb. (1kg) ground turkey

2 TB. chili powder

2 tsp. ground cumin

1 tsp. dried oregano

2 tsp. sea salt

½ tsp. freshly ground black pepper

1 (15-oz.; 420g) can diced tomatoes, with juice

2 (4-oz.; 110g) cans diced green chiles

2 qt. (2l) chicken or vegetable stock

3 small zucchini, trimmed and sliced

5 green onions, white and green parts sliced

½ cup fresh cilantro, chopped

½ cup black olives, pitted and sliced

1. Heat a large skillet over medium-high heat. When hot, add extra-virgin olive oil and wait 30 seconds. Add yellow onion and garlic, and sauté, stirring frequently, for 3 to 5 minutes or until onions are slightly translucent.

2. Add ground turkey, and cook, stirring occasionally, for 5 to 8 minutes or until turkey is lightly browned. Transfer turkey and vegetables to a 6- to 8-quart (5.5- to 7.5-liter) slow cooker.

3. Add chili powder, cumin, oregano, sea salt, black pepper, tomatoes with juice, green chiles, and chicken stock to the slow cooker, and stir with a wooden spoon to combine.

4. Cover and cook on low for 4 hours or on high for 1½ hours.

5. Add zucchini, stir, cover, and cook for 1 or 2 hours.

6. Top with green onions, cilantro, and black olives, and serve.

You can add whatever toppings you like to this chili. Try red onions, avocado, or a dollop of coconut cream, for example.

Green Chili
with Turkey

Turkey Vegetable Meatloaf

Layers of golden sweet potatoes and ground turkey are infused with a variety of garden vegetables and tangy tomato sauce to make a winning combination.

Prep Time	Cook Time
20 minutes	2 or 3 hours
Yield	Serving Size
4 slices	1 slice

Each serving has:

308	28g	9g	29g
calories	carbohydrate	fat	protein

1 large sweet potato, grated

1½ tsp. sea salt

¼ tsp. freshly ground black pepper

2 TB. extra-virgin olive oil

1 small or medium carrot, trimmed and chopped

1 clove garlic

½ medium yellow onion, diced (about ½ cup)

½ medium red bell pepper, ribs and seeds removed, and sliced

3 medium white button mushrooms

½ cup fresh parsley, chopped

1½ tsp. granulated garlic

2 TB. Italian seasoning

1 lb. (450g) ground turkey

3 oz. (85g) tomato paste

½ tsp. raw honey

1. Line the bottom of a 6- to 8-quart (5.5- to 7.5-liter) slow cooker with two pieces of parchment paper.

2. In a medium bowl, toss sweet potatoes in ½ teaspoon sea salt, black pepper, and 1 tablespoon extra-virgin olive oil to fully coat. Place potatoes on the parchment paper in the slow cooker, and gently pat down to cover the entire surface area of the bottom of the crock.

3. Add carrots, garlic, and yellow onion to a large food processor fitted with a chopping blade, and pulse for 15 seconds. Scrape down the sides of the food processor bowl with a rubber scraper.

4. Add red bell pepper, white button mushrooms, parsley, 1 teaspoon granulated garlic, Italian seasoning, remaining 1 tablespoon extra-virgin olive oil, and remaining 1 teaspoon sea salt, and process for 15 seconds or until a chunky paste forms.

5. Transfer vegetable mixture to a large bowl. Add turkey, and mix with a wooden spoon until fully combined.

6. Add turkey-and-vegetable mixture to the slow cooker, and gently press down to cover sweet potatoes.

7. In a small bowl, combine tomato paste, remaining ½ teaspoon granulated garlic, and honey. Using a rubber scraper, spread a thin layer of sauce over top of turkey.

8. Cover and cook on low for 2 or 3 hours or until meatloaf is cooked through and sweet potatoes are tender.

9. Serve warm.

In this mouthwatering dish, succulent duck quarters are browned with allspice and served over a rosemary and orange–scented bed of fennel and apples.

Prep Time	Cook Time
20 minutes	3 to 7 hours
Yield	Serving Size
4 duck quarters	1 quarter

Each serving has:

688 calories	34g carbohydrate	52g fat	26g protein

2 tsp. sea salt

½ tsp. freshly ground black pepper

1 tsp. allspice

1 tsp. granulated garlic

4 (½-lb.; 225g) duck quarters

2 medium fennel bulbs, trimmed and thinly sliced

4 medium apples, peeled, cored, and thinly sliced

1 sprig fresh rosemary

Zest of 1 medium orange (about 2 TB.)

Juice of 1 medium orange

2 TB. extra-virgin olive oil

1 cup chicken or vegetable broth

1. In a small bowl, combine sea salt, black pepper, allspice, and granulated garlic. Rub mixture on all sides of duck quarters. Set aside.

2. In a 6- to 8-quart (5.5- to 7.5-liter) slow cooker, combine fennel, apples, rosemary, orange zest, and orange juice.

3. Heat a large skillet over medium-high heat. When hot, add 1 tablespoon extra-virgin olive oil and wait 30 seconds. Place 2 duck quarters in the skillet, and brown skin for 2 or 3 minutes per side. Transfer quarters to the slow cooker, and repeat with remaining extra-virgin olive oil and duck quarters.

4. Pour chicken broth into the pan, and use a wooden spoon to loosen browned bits. Add chicken broth and browned bits to the slow cooker.

5. Cover and cook on low for 6 or 7 hours, on high for 3 or 4 hours, or until duck reaches an internal temperature of 165°F (75°C) or is done to your liking.

6. If you prefer, remove skin and fat cap from duck before serving over a scoop of fennel and apples. Or for a crisper skin, broil duck, fat side up, for 1 or 2 minutes before serving.

You can easily substitute 4 large (6-ounce; 170-gram) duck breasts instead of using full duck quarters in this recipe.

Duck Quarters
with Fennel and Apples

Chapter 7

Pork Dishes

Slow cooked pork is hard to resist when it's seasoned to perfection and ready to fall off the bone. The recipes in this chapter call for a variety of cuts, including ham hocks, shoulder, sausages, and bacon. Feel free to use substitutions if you prefer to eliminate all cured meats—they could include small amounts of sugar from the brine. Pork is also a very fatty meat to cook. Trimming excess fat before browning or skimming excess fat off the top of the cooking liquid before serving can help reduce the fat content of the finished dish.

Pork Broth

This smoky, dense, and earthy broth, accentuated with mushrooms and cabbage, makes a wonderful, deep base for soups or stews.

Prep Time	Cook Time
10 minutes	8 to 24 hours
Yield	Serving Size
4 quarts (4 liters)	2 cups

Each serving has:			
81 calories	2g carbohydrate	6g fat	7g protein

2 lb. (1kg) ham hocks (about 2 large hocks)

2 shallots, halved

2 cloves garlic, crushed

½ medium green cabbage, sliced

8 sprigs fresh parsley

6 dried shiitake mushrooms

1 TB. sea salt

1 tsp. whole black peppercorns

½ tsp. whole coriander seeds

1 bay leaf

Juice of 1 medium lemon

5 qt. (4.75l) water

1. In a 6- to 8-quart (5.5- to 7.5-liter) slow cooker, combine ham hocks, shallots, garlic, green cabbage, parsley, shiitake mushrooms, sea salt, black peppercorns, coriander seeds, bay leaf, lemon juice, and water.

2. Cover and cook on low for 8 to 24 hours.

3. Strain through a fine sieve to separate ham hocks and vegetables from broth. Discard vegetables, and remove meat from ham hocks. (Save meat for later use, if desired.)

4. Use broth immediately as a base for soups or stews, or freeze in portions for later use.

Pork bones aren't often used for bone broth in the same way chicken and beef bones are. Instead, this recipe uses a large ham hock, so some of the natural flavor from the bone will be extracted.

Savory pork flavors combine with sweet butternut squash in this rich winter stew. Leafy greens and lemon juice add a brightness that cuts through the dark broth.

Prep Time	Cook Time
30 minutes	7 or 8 hours

Yield	Serving Size
4 quarts (4 liters)	2½ cups

Each serving has:

501 calories	34g carbohydrate	30g fat	29g protein

1 lb. (450g) spicy Italian sausage links, sliced

2 cloves garlic, minced

1 large yellow onion, diced

2 medium carrots, peeled, trimmed, and diced

2 qt. (2l) chicken or vegetable stock

1 lb. (450g) ham hock (about 1 large hock)

½ small butternut squash, diced (4 cups)

1 tsp. sea salt

½ tsp. freshly ground black pepper

1 lb. (450g) bunch kale, chopped and woody stems removed

Juice of ½ medium lemon

1. Heat a medium skillet over medium-high heat. When hot, add Italian sausage links, and cook, stirring frequently, for 3 to 5 minutes or until browned. Remove sausage and refrigerate for later use.

2. Add garlic, yellow onion, and carrots to the skillet, and sauté, stirring frequently, in residual sausage grease for 3 to 5 minutes, until onions are softened and slightly translucent.

3. Add ½ cup chicken stock, and use a wooden spoon to loosen browned bits. Pour chicken stock and browned bits into a 6- to 8-quart (5.5- to 7.5-liter) slow cooker.

4. Add ham hock, butternut squash, sea salt, black pepper, and remaining 7½ cups chicken stock.

5. Cover and cook on low for 6 or 7 hours.

6. 30 minutes before serving, transfer ham hock to a cutting board. When it's cool enough to touch, carefully discard cartilage and bone, and return ham to the slow cooker.

7. Add refrigerated sausage slices, kale, and lemon juice, and stir to combine.

8. Cover and cook for 10 more minutes.

9. Taste stew, and season with additional sea salt if desired. Ladle into large bowls, and serve hot.

Your grocery store might not have ham hocks on display, but most butchers have them in the back. Any piece of bone-in ham works for this recipe if you can't track down a hock.

Italian Pork and Vegetable Stew

Easy Pulled Pork

In this mouthwatering dish, succulent, paprika-rubbed pork shoulder is slow cooked in apple juice and served over a hearty helping of leafy greens.

Prep Time	Cook Time
20 minutes	4 to 8 hours, plus marinade time
Yield	Serving Size
4 cups	1 cup

Each serving has:

483 calories	12g carbohydrate	17g fat	66g protein

2 tsp. sea salt

1 tsp. freshly ground black pepper

1 TB. smoked paprika

2 lb. (1kg) boneless pork shoulder

2 TB. coconut oil or bacon drippings

1 medium yellow onion, diced

1 cup unsweetened apple juice, or juice of 2 medium apples

2 TB. apple cider vinegar

Juice of 1 medium lemon

8 cups baby spinach

1. In a small bowl, combine sea salt, black pepper, and smoked paprika. Rub mixture on all sides of pork shoulder.

2. Put pork shoulder in a bowl or shallow dish, cover with plastic wrap, and refrigerate overnight.

3. The next day, heat a medium skillet over medium-high heat. When hot, add coconut oil and wait 30 seconds. Add pork to the pan, and brown on all sides for about 1 or 2 minutes per side. Transfer pork to a 4- or 5-quart (4- to 5-liter) slow cooker.

4. Add yellow onion to the pan, and sauté, stirring frequently, for 3 to 5 minutes or until slightly translucent.

5. Use a wooden spoon to loosen browned bits on the bottom of the pan, and place onions over pork shoulder in the slow cooker.

6. Add apple juice and apple cider vinegar to the slow cooker.

7. Cover and cook on high for 4 to 6 hours, on low for 6 to 8 hours, or until pork reaches an internal temperature of at least 145°F (65°C) and is tender.

8. Using two metal forks, shred pork shoulder into small pieces.

9. Add lemon juice, adjust sea salt if needed, cover, and cook for 20 minutes.

10. To serve, scoop hot pork shoulder with juices over a bed of baby spinach.

The distinct taste of juniper freshens up this rich combination of smoked bacon, tender pork shoulder, and zesty kielbasa served over caraway-studded sauerkraut.

Prep Time **20 minutes**	Cook Time **4 to 8 hours**
Yield **12 cups**	Serving Size **2 cups**

Each serving has:

646 calories	**10g** carbohydrate	**20g** fat	**59g** protein

8 juniper berries, crushed

6 whole black peppercorns

1 whole clove

2 tsp. sea salt

2 lb. (1kg) pork shoulder

4 slices bacon, cut into 1-in. (2.5cm) pieces

1 medium yellow onion, diced

1 medium carrot, trimmed, peeled, and diced

2 cloves garlic, minced

1¼ cups dry white wine

2 lb. (1kg) fresh sauerkraut, drained

1 tsp. caraway seeds

2 bay leaves

1 lb. (450g) ring kielbasa

1. Place juniper berries, black peppercorns, and clove in the center of a 6-inch (15-centimeter) square of cheesecloth. Bring up corners and tie into a bundle, ensuring spices are contained and won't fall out. Set aside.

2. Rub sea salt on all sides of pork shoulder. Set aside.

3. Heat a medium skillet over medium heat. When hot, add bacon and cook, turning frequently, for 8 to 10 minutes or until crisp. Remove bacon from the pan, and set aside.

4. Place pork in the pan, and brown for about 1 or 2 minutes per side. Transfer pork to a 6- to 8-quart (5.5- to 7.5-liter) slow cooker.

5. Add yellow onion, carrot, and garlic to the pan, and sauté, stirring frequently, for 5 to 7 minutes or until onions are slightly translucent.

6. Add ¼ cup white wine to the hot skillet, and use a wooden spoon to loosen browned bits. Pour wine and browned bits over pork shoulder in the slow cooker.

7. Add cooked bacon, sauerkraut, and caraway seeds to the slow cooker, and mix together with a wooden spoon around pork shoulder.

8. Bury bay leaves and cheesecloth spice sachet in sauerkraut. Pour remaining 1 cup white wine over top.

9. Cover and cook on high for 4 to 6 hours, on low for 6 to 8 hours, or until pork reaches an internal temperature of at least 145°F (65°C) and is tender.

10. 20 minutes before serving, remove bay leaves and cheesecloth sachet, and add kielbasa. Cover and continue to cook until kielbasa is warmed.

Choucroute Garnie
(Pork with Sauerkraut)

Ham Hocks
with Collard Greens

This simple dish—salted pork shank with rosemary and a hint of lemon served over tender collard greens—is loaded with savory flavor.

Prep Time	Cook Time
15 minutes	4 to 8 hours
Yield	Serving Size
8 cups	2 cups

Each serving has:

295	17g	18g	21g
calories	carbohydrate	fat	protein

2 lb. (1kg) collard greens, stems removed and roughly chopped

2 tsp. sea salt

1 tsp. freshly ground black pepper

2 lb. (1kg) ham hocks (about 2 large hocks)

1 TB. extra-virgin olive oil

½ medium yellow onion, diced

1 medium carrot, trimmed, peeled, and diced

2 cloves garlic, crushed

2 cups pork or chicken stock

1 (6-in.; 15cm) fresh rosemary sprig

Juice of 1 medium lemon

1. Place collard greens in the bottom of a 6- to 8-quart (5.5- to 7.5-liter) slow cooker.

2. In a small bowl, combine sea salt and black pepper. Rub mixture on all sides of ham hocks.

3. Heat a medium skillet over medium-high heat. When hot, add extra-virgin olive oil and wait 30 seconds. Add ham hocks to the pan, and brown for about 30 seconds to 1 minute per side. Remove ham hocks from the pan and nestle among collard greens in the slow cooker.

4. Add yellow onion to the skillet, and sauté, stirring frequently, for 3 to 5 minutes or until slightly translucent.

5. Add carrot and garlic, and cook, stirring occasionally, for 3 to 5 minutes. Transfer vegetables to the slow cooker over ham hocks.

6. Add ¼ cup pork stock to the pan, and use a wooden spoon to loosen browned bits. Pour pork stock and browned bits into the slow cooker.

7. Add remaining 1¾ cups pork stock and rosemary to the slow cooker.

8. Cover and cook on high for 4 to 6 hours, on low for 6 to 8 hours, or until pork reaches an internal temperature of at least 145°F (65°C) and is tender.

9. Drizzle with lemon juice, and serve.

Cardamom stars in this deceptively simple pork and squash dish. Known as the queen of spices because of its exotic flavor, cardamom adds a warm, sweet, penetrating aroma that's hard to resist.

	Prep Time	Cook Time
	20 minutes	4 to 8 hours
	Yield	Serving Size
	9 cups	1½ cups

Each serving has:

466 calories	9g carbohydrate	34g fat	30g protein

2 tsp. sea salt

1 tsp. freshly ground black pepper

1 TB. ground cardamom

1 tsp. ground cumin

3 lb. (1.5kg) pork shoulder

2 TB. coconut oil

1 large shallot, diced

¼ cup fresh sage leaves, chopped

¼ cup pork or vegetable stock

1 small (3-lb.; 1.5kg) butternut squash, peeled and diced

1. In a small bowl, combine sea salt, black pepper, cardamom, and cumin. Rub mixture on all sides of pork shoulder.

2. Heat a medium skillet over medium-high heat. When hot, add coconut oil and wait 30 seconds. Add pork to the pan, and brown for about 1 or 2 minutes per side. Transfer pork to a 4- or 5-quart (4- to 5-liter) slow cooker.

3. Add shallot and sage leaves to the pan, and sauté, stirring frequently, for 3 to 5 minutes or until shallots are slightly translucent.

4. Add pork stock to the pan, and use a wooden spoon to loosen browned bits. Pour pork stock and browned bits over pork shoulder in the slow cooker.

5. Add butternut squash over top.

6. Cover and cook on high for 4 to 6 hours, on low for 6 to 8 hours, or until pork reaches an internal temperature of at least 145°F (65°C) and is tender.

7. Slice pork, and serve warm.

Instead of the peeled and diced butternut squash, you can substitute 3 pounds (1.5 kilograms) diced yams or sweet potatoes.

Braised Pork Shoulder
with Sage and Butternut Squash

Sausage
with Leeks and Tomatoes

Leeks add a creaminess to balance the acidity of the tomatoes and spicy punch of the sausage in this hearty dish.

Prep Time	Cook Time
15 minutes	3 to 6 hours
Yield	Serving Size
8 cups	2 cups

Each serving has:

509 calories	38g carbohydrate	30g fat	21g protein

2 TB. coconut oil

3 medium leeks, white and light green parts chopped

1 lb. (450g) ground Italian pork sausage

1 (28-oz.; 800g) can fire-roasted crushed tomatoes, with juice

Juice of ½ medium lemon

1 TB. Italian seasoning

½ tsp. granulated garlic

½ tsp. crushed red pepper flakes (optional)

2 tsp. sea salt

1½ lb. (680g) cauliflower florets (about 1 large head)

1. Heat a medium skillet over medium-high heat. When hot, add coconut oil and wait 30 seconds. Add leeks, and sauté, stirring frequently, for 3 to 5 minutes or until slightly translucent.

2. Add Italian pork sausage, and cook, stirring occasionally, for 3 minutes or until meat begins to brown. Transfer leeks and browned sausage to a 4- or 5-quart (4- to 5-liter) slow cooker.

3. Pour ¼ cup juice from fire-roasted crushed tomatoes into the pan, and use a wooden spoon to loosen browned bits. Pour tomato juice and browned bits into the slow cooker.

4. Add remaining tomatoes and juice, lemon juice, Italian seasoning, granulated garlic, crushed red pepper flakes (if using), and sea salt to the slow cooker, and stir with a wooden spoon.

5. Add cauliflower on top.

6. Cover and cook on high for 3 or 4 hours or on low for 4 to 6 hours.

7. Serve warm.

If you can't find seasoned Italian pork sausage, you can substitute ground pork, chicken, or beef, but you'll need to increase the Italian seasoning, granulated garlic, and sea salt to taste.

This pork shoulder dish gets its flavor from the warm, nutty, citrus taste of coriander; bold red wine; tangy lemon slices; and salty, mouthwatering kalamata olives.

Prep Time	Cook Time
15 minutes	4 to 8 hours, plus marinade time
Yield	Serving Size
4 cups	1 cup

Each serving has:

735 calories	7g carbohydrate	20g fat	65g protein

1 tsp. sea salt

½ tsp. freshly ground black pepper

2 TB. whole coriander seeds, lightly crushed

2 lb. (1kg) pork shoulder

2 TB. extra-virgin olive oil

1 cup red wine

3 cloves garlic, sliced

1 (2-in.; 2.5cm) cinnamon stick

1 bay leaf

1 medium lemon, thinly sliced

1 cup kalamata olives

1. In a small bowl, combine sea salt, black pepper, and coriander seeds. Rub mixture on all sides of pork shoulder.

2. Put pork in a bowl or shallow dish, cover with plastic wrap, and refrigerate overnight.

3. The next day, heat a medium skillet over medium-high heat. When hot, add extra-virgin olive oil and wait 30 seconds. Add pork to the pan, and brown for about 1 or 2 minutes per side. Transfer pork to a 4- or 5-quart (4- to 5-liter) slow cooker.

4. Add red wine to the skillet, and use a wooden spoon to loosen browned bits. Pour red wine and browned bits into the slow cooker over pork.

5. Add garlic, cinnamon stick, and bay leaf to the slow cooker.

6. Cover and cook on high for 4 to 6 hours, on low for 6 to 8 hours, or until pork reaches an internal temperature of 145°F (65°C).

7. Remove bay leaf, slice pork, and serve with lemon slices and kalamata olives.

The crushed coriander seeds can be a bit gritty in this recipe. If you'd prefer, use ground coriander instead. The flavor won't be quite as pungent, but it will still be delicious.

Afelia
(Spiced Pork with Coriander and Red Wine)

Paleo Ramen

Bacon fat, coconut aminos, and shiitake mushrooms add richness and depth to this pork stock soup. Bright zucchini ribbons bring an unexpected freshness and crunch.

Prep Time	Cook Time
20 minutes	4 to 8 hours
Yield	Serving Size
2½ quarts (2.5 liters)	3 cups

Each serving has:			
320 calories	28g carbohydrate	17g fat	18g protein

2 qt. (2l) pork stock

¼ cup coconut aminos

1 TB. pure grade B maple syrup

6 dried shiitake mushrooms

1 (1-in.; 2.5cm) piece gingerroot, peeled and halved

8 to 10 scallions, white and light green parts sliced thin

1 lb. (450g) ham hock

4 medium zucchini

4 heads baby bok choy, or 1 medium head, sliced

4 (6×3-in.; 15×8cm) sheets nori, cut into strips

4 large hard-boiled eggs, peeled and halved

1. In a 4- or 5-quart (4- to 5-liter) slow cooker, whisk together pork stock, coconut aminos, and maple syrup.

2. Add shiitake mushrooms, gingerroot, 6 scallions, and ham hock.

3. Cover and cook on high for 4 to 8 hours or on low for 6 to 12 hours. (You can't overcook stock at this point, so leave it on as long as you can to get the richest flavor.)

4. Meanwhile, using a vegetable peeler, peel zucchini lengthwise to create noodlelike ribbons. Refrigerate for later use.

5. 10 minutes before mealtime, remove ham hock from the slow cooker and place on a cutting board to cool. Also, remove and discard gingerroot.

6. Add baby bok choy to the slow cooker.

7. Cover and cook for 10 minutes.

8. When ham hock is cool enough to touch, carefully discard cartilage and bone, and return meaty portions to soup.

9. To serve, ladle broth over a bowl of zucchini ribbons, and top with ham, bok choy, remaining 2 to 4 scallions, nori, and hard-boiled eggs.

Nori is a thin sheet of seaweed, and you can find it at most larger grocery stores. If you can't find nori, you can use any type of seaweed to give this dish a flavor and nutrition boost.

Chapter 8

Beef and Game Mains

Low and slow is the perfect cooking method for beef and game, especially tougher cuts. Whether you're looking for a simple ground beef dinner option or a way to prepare that brisket in the freezer, this chapter will inspire you. Remember to opt for grass-fed or pasture-raised beef, if you can find it, and feel free to substitute a similar cut of wild game for beef in any of the recipes for a nice variation.

Caramelized beef bones produce a rich, hearty-flavored broth, accentuated by black pepper and rosemary.

Prep Time	Cook Time
60 minutes	9 to 25 hours
Yield	Serving Size
4 quarts (4 liters)	2 cups

Each serving has:

81 calories	0g carbohydrate	6g fat	8g protein

2 lb. (1kg) beef bones

1 large yellow onion, quartered

4 cloves garlic, crushed

3 medium carrots, sliced

2 large stalks celery, sliced

1 TB. sea salt

1 tsp. whole black peppercorns

2 bay leaves

1 sprig fresh rosemary

2 TB. apple cider vinegar

5 qt. (4.75l) water

1. Preheat the oven to 400°F (200°C).

2. Arrange beef bones on a metal baking sheet, and bake for 45 minutes.

3. Meanwhile, in a 6- to 8-quart (5.5- to 7.5-liter) slow cooker, combine yellow onion, garlic, carrots, celery, sea salt, black peppercorns, bay leaves, rosemary, apple cider vinegar, and water.

4. Add roasted beef bones when they're ready.

5. Cover and cook on low for 8 to 24 hours.

6. Strain through a fine sieve to separate bones and vegetables from broth. Discard bones and vegetables.

7. Use broth immediately as a base for soups or stews, or freeze for later use.

It's okay if you don't have time to roast the bones ahead of time. However, this step does add a richness and depth of flavor that cannot be achieved unless the bones are caramelized from the oven's high temperatures.

Beef Bone Broth

Beef and Vegetable Chili

Tender chunks of chipotle-spiced beef intermingle with zucchini, red bell pepper, mushrooms, and a hearty helping of kale in this rich chili.

Prep Time	Cook Time
30 minutes	3 to 8 hours
Yield	Serving Size
4 quarts (4 liters)	2 cups

Each serving has:

320 calories	15g carbohydrate	18g fat	25g protein

2 TB. chili or chipotle powder

1 TB. sea salt

1 tsp. ground cumin

1 tsp. granulated garlic

2 lb. (1kg) beef stew meat

2 TB. coconut oil

1 large yellow onion, diced

2 (28-oz.; 800g) cans diced tomatoes, with juice

2 (4-oz.; 110g) cans diced green chiles, with liquid

8 medium white button mushrooms, sliced

½ tsp. dried oregano

4 medium green or yellow zucchini, trimmed and diced

1 large red bell pepper, ribs and seeds removed, and diced

6 large kale leaves, woody stems removed, and chopped

½ cup fresh cilantro, chopped

1 medium avocado, peeled, pitted, and sliced

1 (14-fl. oz.; 400ml) can full-fat coconut milk, chilled

1. In a medium bowl, combine chili powder, sea salt, cumin, and granulated garlic.

2. Add beef stew meat, and stir or toss until completely coated with spice mixture.

3. Heat a large skillet over medium-high heat. When hot, add 1 tablespoon coconut oil and wait 30 seconds. Add enough beef stew meat to cover the bottom of the pan, and cook, turning as needed, for 3 to 5 minutes or until browned. Transfer browned beef to a 6- to 8-quart (5.5- to 7.5-liter) slow cooker. Repeat with remaining 1 tablespoon coconut oil and beef stew meat.

4. Add yellow onion to the skillet, and sauté, stirring frequently, for 3 to 5 minutes or until slightly translucent. Transfer onion to the slow cooker.

5. Pour ¼ cup juice from tomatoes into the skillet, and use a wooden spoon to loosen browned bits. Add tomato juice and browned bits to the slow cooker.

6. Add diced tomatoes and remaining juice, green chiles, white button mushrooms, and oregano to the slow cooker, and stir.

7. Cover and cook on high for 2 hours or on low for 5 hours.

8. Add zucchini, red bell pepper, and kale, and stir.

9. Cover and cook for 1 or 2 more hours on the same temperature used earlier or until beef is tender.

10. To serve, garnish with fresh cilantro, avocado, and a spoonful of coconut cream from the top of the can.

This recipe combines seasoned oxtails, the meaty tails of beef, with fennel, garlic, and shallots. Dried figs, a hint of cinnamon, and allspice add a touch of sweet warmth.

Prep Time	Cook Time
30 minutes	3 to 8 hours
Yield	Serving Size
3 quarts (3 liters)	2 cups

Each serving has:			
350 calories	26g carbohydrate	16g fat	17g protein

¼ tsp. allspice

1 TB. sea salt

½ tsp. freshly ground black pepper

3 lb. (1.5kg) oxtails

3 tsp. extra-virgin olive oil

2 medium shallots, diced

4 cups beef broth

4 cloves garlic, crushed

2 medium carrots, trimmed, peeled, and sliced

2 large stalks celery, sliced

1½ lb. (680g) fennel bulbs, trimmed and sliced

8 dried figs, stems removed, and halved

2 fresh sprigs rosemary

1 (1-in.; 2.5cm) cinnamon stick

1 bay leaf

1 tsp. lemon zest

1. In a medium bowl, combine allspice, sea salt, and black pepper.

2. Add oxtails, and stir or toss until completely coated with spice mixture.

3. Heat a large skillet over medium-high heat. When hot, add 1 teaspoon extra-virgin olive oil and wait 30 seconds. Add enough oxtails to cover the bottom of the pan, and cook, turning as needed, for 3 to 5 minutes or until browned. Transfer browned oxtails to a 4- or 5-quart (4- to 5-liter) slow cooker. Repeat with any remaining oxtails and 1 teaspoon extra-virgin olive oil.

4. Add remaining 1 teaspoon extra-virgin olive oil and shallots to the skillet, and sauté, stirring frequently, for 3 to 5 minutes or until slightly translucent. Transfer shallots to the slow cooker.

5. Pour ¼ cup beef broth into the skillet, and use a wooden spoon to loosen browned bits. Add beef broth and browned bits to the slow cooker.

6. Add garlic, carrots, celery, fennel, figs, rosemary, cinnamon stick, bay leaf, lemon zest, and remaining 3¾ cups beef broth to the slow cooker, and stir.

7. Cover and cook on high for 3 or 4 hours, on low for 6 to 8 hours, or until oxtails are tender and fall off the bone.

8. Remove cinnamon stick, and bay leaf, and serve hot.

Braised Oxtail Stew

Pho
(Vietnamese Beef Soup)

In this vibrant soup, rich beef broth combines with fresh herbs and vegetables. Traditionally, the toppings are served separately and can be added however you like.

Prep Time	Cook Time
20 minutes	4 to 12 hours
Yield	Serving Size
2½ quarts (2.5 liters)	3 cups

Each serving has:			
551 calories	14g carbohydrate	31g fat	52g protein

1 cardamom pod

1 star anise

1 whole clove

2 tsp. whole coriander seeds

2 qt. (2l) beef stock

1 (2-in.; 5cm) piece gingerroot, peeled and halved

4 medium zucchini

2 TB. sesame oil

1 lb. (450g) beef flank steak

1 tsp. sea salt

2 cups fresh mung bean sprouts

1 medium red bell pepper, ribs and seeds removed, and sliced

2 small limes, cut into wedges

½ cup fresh mint or cilantro, chopped

Hot pepper sauce (optional)

1. Place cardamom pod, star anise, clove, and coriander seeds in the center of a 6-inch (15-centimeter) square of cheesecloth. Bring up corners and tie into a bundle, ensuring spices are contained and won't fall out.

2. Add beef stock, gingerroot, and spice sachet to a 4- or 5-quart (4- to 5-liter) slow cooker.

3. Cover and cook on high for 4 to 8 hours or on low for 6 to 12 hours. (Stock cannot be overcooked at this point, so leave it on as long as you want to get the richest flavor.)

4. Meanwhile, using a vegetable peeler, peel zucchini lengthwise to create noodlelike ribbons. Refrigerate for later use.

5. 15 minutes before mealtime, heat a large skillet over medium-high heat. When hot, add sesame oil and wait 30 seconds.

6. Season beef flank steak with sea salt. Add to the skillet, and sear on all sides for about 1 minute per side.

7. Place seared steak on a cutting board, and slice against the grain into ¼-inch (1-centimeter) slices. Set aside.

8. Remove gingerroot and spice sachet from the slow cooker, and add steak.

9. Cover and cook for 2 to 5 minutes or until beef is cooked to your liking.

10. To serve, ladle broth over a bowl of zucchini ribbons. Top with mung bean sprouts, red bell pepper slices, lime wedge, mint, and hot pepper sauce (if using).

In this Paleo version of the classic recipe, tender beef is slow cooked in red wine with onions, mushrooms, and sunchokes.

Prep Time	Cook Time
20 minutes	3 to 7 hours
Yield	Serving Size
12 cups	2 cups

Each serving has:

530	16g	29g	29g
calories	carbohydrate	fat	protein

2 tsp. sea salt

½ tsp. freshly ground black pepper

2 lb. (1kg) beef stew meat, cut into 1-in. (2.5cm) cubes

2 slices bacon, finely diced

2 cups red wine

1 bay leaf

½ tsp. dried thyme

½ tsp. dried parsley

6 to 8 pearl onions, peeled and halved

2 cloves garlic, sliced

1 medium carrot, trimmed, peeled, and sliced

1 lb. (450g) medium white button mushrooms, quartered

½ lb. (225g) sunchokes, peeled and diced

1. In a medium bowl, combine sea salt and black pepper.

2. Add beef stew meat, and stir or toss until completely coated with spice mixture. Set aside.

3. Heat a large skillet over medium-high heat. When hot, add bacon, and cook, stirring frequently, for 4 to 6 minutes or until bacon is browned and crisp. Remove bacon from the pan, and reserve bacon fat.

4. Add 1 tablespoon bacon fat back to the skillet, and return skillet to heat. When hot, add enough beef cubes to cover the bottom of the pan. Cook, turning as needed, for 3 to 5 minutes or until browned. Transfer browned beef to a 4- or 5-quart (4- to 5-liter) slow cooker. Repeat with remaining stew meat.

5. Pour ¼ cup red wine into the skillet, and use a wooden spoon to loosen browned bits. Add red wine and browned bits to the slow cooker.

6. Add remaining 1¾ cups red wine, bay leaf, thyme, parsley, pearl onions, garlic, and carrot to the slow cooker, and stir.

7. Cover and cook on high for 3 hours or on low for 5 hours.

8. Remove the lid, stir, and add white button mushrooms and sunchokes.

9. Cover and cook for 2 or 3 hours or until beef and vegetables are tender.

10. Remove bay leaf before serving hot.

Beef Bourguignon

Shredded Beef Tacos

Spiced beef is shredded in its own cooking juices and layered on top of crisp lettuce leaves with salsa and creamy avocado in this easy dinnertime staple.

Prep Time	Cook Time
20 minutes	4 to 10 hours
Yield	Serving Size
4 cups	1 cup

Each serving has:			
697 calories	10g carbohydrate	43g fat	68g protein

3 lb. (1.5kg) beef chuck roast

1 TB. sea salt

½ tsp. freshly ground black pepper

1 TB. extra-virgin olive oil

1 medium yellow onion, diced

2 cups beef broth

1 TB. chili powder

1 tsp. ground cumin

1 tsp. granulated garlic

1 head green leaf or romaine lettuce

½ cup fresh cilantro, chopped

1 medium avocado, pitted and sliced

1 cup fresh salsa

1. Rub beef chuck roast on all sides with sea salt and black pepper.

2. Heat a medium skillet over medium-high heat. When hot, add extra-virgin olive oil and wait 30 seconds. Add roast to the skillet, and cook for 3 to 5 minutes or until browned. Turn roast, and repeat browning on all sides. Transfer browned beef to a 4- or 5-quart (4- to 5-liter) slow cooker.

3. Add yellow onion to the skillet, and sauté, stirring frequently, for 3 to 5 minutes or until slightly translucent. Transfer onion to the slow cooker.

4. Pour ¼ cup beef broth into the skillet, and use a wooden spoon to loosen browned bits. Add beef broth and browned bits to the slow cooker.

5. Sprinkle roast with chili powder, cumin, and granulated garlic, and pour remaining 1¾ cups beef broth over top.

6. Cover and cook on low for 8 to 10 hours, on high for 4 to 6 hours, or until tender.

7. Use two metal forks to shred beef in the slow cooker, and season with additional sea salt if needed.

8. To serve, place a hearty spoonful of shredded beef in the center of 1 lettuce leaf. Top with cilantro, avocado, and salsa, fold lettuce over into wrap, and serve.

Variation: To make **Shredded Chicken Tacos,** replace the beef chuck roast with 3 pounds (1.5 kilograms) boneless, skinless chicken breasts. Cook on low for 5 or 6 hours, on high for 3 or 4 hours, or until chicken reaches an internal temperature of 165°F (75°C) and is fork-tender.

Tart blackberries make a perfect substitute for sugar-filled barbecue sauce on these slow cooked short ribs. They're excellent served alongside a tossed green salad.

	Prep Time	Cook Time
	20 minutes	4 to 8 hours
	Yield	Serving Size
	8 cups	1 cup

Each serving has:			
760 calories	14g carbohydrate	44g fat	73g protein

1 tsp. sea salt

½ tsp. freshly ground black pepper

1 TB. paprika

1 TB. granulated garlic

2 TB. coconut oil, melted

¼ cup balsamic vinegar

1 TB. raw honey

4 lb. (2kg) beef short ribs

1 lb. (450g) frozen blackberries

1 cup beef broth

1. In a large bowl, combine sea salt, black pepper, paprika, granulated garlic, melted coconut oil, balsamic vinegar, and honey.

2. Add beef short ribs, and toss to coat.

3. Place blackberries and beef broth in a 4- or 5-quart (4- to 5-liter) slow cooker. Add ribs and any remaining marinade in the bowl.

4. Cover and cook on low for 6 to 8 hours, on high for 4 or 5 hours, or until ribs are fully cooked.

5. Using a strainer, separate ribs from remaining cooking liquid. Add liquid to a medium skillet, and set over high heat.

6. Cook liquid, stirring constantly, for 3 or 4 minutes or until it reduces and thickens slightly to a glaze. Remove from heat, and season with additional sea salt if needed.

7. Drizzle glaze over short ribs, and serve.

It's important not to oversalt this recipe early on. The cooking juices reduce drastically, and the salt, therefore, is more concentrated. Taste the sauce right before serving and adjust salt then as needed.

Blackberry-Glazed Short Ribs

Five-Spice Beef

In this hearty dish, warm Chinese five-spice flavors beef stew meat that's tossed with carrots and lightly steamed broccoli.

Prep Time	Cook Time
20 minutes	3 to 8 hours
Yield	Serving Size
10 cups	2 cups

Each serving has:

545	14g	39g	34g
calories	carbohydrate	fat	protein

1 TB. Chinese five-spice powder

½ tsp. granulated garlic

2 tsp. sea salt

2 lb. (1kg) beef stew meat, cut into 1-in. (2.5cm) cubes

2 TB. coconut oil

4 cups beef broth

1 large yellow onion, diced

4 large carrots, trimmed, peeled, and sliced

1 lb. (450g) fresh broccoli florets

1. In a medium bowl, combine Chinese five-spice powder, granulated garlic, and sea salt.

2. Add beef stew meat, and stir or toss until completely coated with spice mixture.

3. Heat a large skillet over medium-high heat. When hot, add 1 tablespoon coconut oil and wait 30 seconds. Add enough beef cubes to cover the bottom of the pan, and cook, turning as needed, for 3 to 5 minutes or until browned. Transfer browned beef to a 4- or 5-quart (4- to 5-liter) slow cooker. Repeat with remaining beef stew meat.

4. Pour ¼ cup beef broth into the skillet, and use a wooden spoon to loosen browned bits. Add beef broth and browned bits to the slow cooker.

5. Return the skillet to medium-high heat. When hot, add remaining 1 tablespoon coconut oil and wait 30 seconds. Add yellow onion to the skillet, and sauté, stirring frequently, for 3 to 5 minutes or until slightly translucent. Transfer onion to the slow cooker.

6. Add remaining 3¾ cups beef broth and carrots to the slow cooker, and stir.

7. Cover and cook on high for 3 hours or on low for 5 hours.

8. Remove the lid, stir, and add broccoli florets.

9. Cover and cook for 1 or 2 hours or until beef and vegetables are tender.

10. Stir with a wooden spoon before serving warm.

Succulent paprika-rubbed brisket is slow cooked in sauerkraut, fresh apples, and peppery bacon.

	Prep Time		Cook Time
	40 minutes		**4 to 10 hours**
	Yield		Serving Size
	12 cups		**1½ cups**

Each serving has:

697	11g	48g	50g
calories	carbohydrate	fat	protein

¼ lb. (125g) pepper bacon, diced

1 medium yellow onion, diced

1 clove garlic, minced

1 medium apple, cored and diced

2 cups beef broth

2 lb. (1kg) fresh sauerkraut, drained

1 tsp. caraway seeds

2 tsp. sea salt

½ tsp. freshly ground black pepper

1 tsp. smoked paprika

¼ tsp. ground cinnamon

3 lb. (1.5kg) beef brisket

1 TB. extra-virgin olive oil

1. Heat a medium skillet over medium heat. When hot, add pepper bacon, and cook, stirring frequently, for 8 to 10 minutes or until crisp. Transfer bacon to a 6- to 8-quart (5.5- to 7.5-liter) slow cooker.

2. Add yellow onion and garlic to the skillet, and sauté in bacon fat, stirring frequently, for 5 to 7 minutes or until onions are slightly translucent.

3. Add apple, and cook for 5 minutes. Transfer contents of skillet to the slow cooker.

4. Add ¼ cup beef broth to the hot skillet, and use a wooden spoon to loosen browned bits. Add broth and browned bits to the slow cooker.

5. Add sauerkraut, caraway seeds, and ½ teaspoon sea salt to the slow cooker, and stir with a wooden spoon to combine.

6. In a small bowl, combine remaining 1½ teaspoons sea salt, black pepper, smoked paprika, and cinnamon. Rub mixture on all sides of beef brisket.

7. Set the skillet over medium-high heat. When hot, add extra-virgin olive oil and wait 30 seconds. Add spice-rubbed brisket to the pan, fatty side down, and brown for 3 to 5 minutes or until dark golden brown. Turn over brisket and brown on the other side. Transfer brisket to the slow cooker, and nestle in sauerkraut mixture.

8. Pour remaining 1¾ cups beef broth over top.

9. Cover and cook on high for 4 or 5 hours, on low for 8 to 10 hours, or until beef reaches an internal temperature of at least 145°F (63°C) and is tender.

10. Slice brisket against the grain and serve alongside a hearty scoop of sauerkraut and apples.

Beef Brisket
with Sauerkraut and Apples

Spaghetti
with Bison Meatballs

In this tasty dish, spaghetti squash "noodles" are coated with a full-bodied, peppery tomato sauce and topped with bacon and bison meatballs.

Prep Time	Cook Time
20 minutes	4 to 8 hours
Yield	Serving Size
4 cups squash and 16 meatballs	1 cup squash and 4 meatballs

Each serving has:			
315 calories	44g carbohydrate	12g fat	9g protein

1 (28-oz.; 800g) can tomato sauce

1 tsp. granulated garlic

2 tsp. Italian seasoning blend

¼ tsp. crushed red pepper flakes (optional)

3 tsp. sea salt

¼ tsp. freshly ground black pepper

½ tsp. coconut aminos

2 cloves garlic, crushed

1 medium shallot, diced

2 large eggs

2 slices bacon (about 2 oz.)

1 TB. coconut flour

½ tsp. dried oregano

2 lb. (1kg) ground bison

2 TB. extra-virgin olive oil

½ lb. (225g) white button mushrooms, sliced

1 small spaghetti squash

1. In a 6- to 8-quart (5.5- to 7.5-liter) slow cooker, combine tomato sauce, granulated garlic, Italian seasoning blend, crushed red pepper flakes (if using), 2 teaspoons sea salt, black pepper, and coconut aminos, and stir with a wooden spoon.

2. Cover and set the slow cooker on high.

3. In a food processor fitted with a chopping blade, pulse garlic, shallot, and remaining 1 teaspoon sea salt for 30 seconds or until rough paste forms.

4. Add eggs, bacon, coconut flour, and oregano, and pulse for 30 seconds or until blended.

5. Place bison in a large bowl, add contents of the food processor, and use a wooden spoon to combine. Form bison mixture into 16 meatballs.

6. Heat a medium skillet over medium-high heat. When hot, add 1 tablespoon extra-virgin olive oil and wait 30 seconds. Add 8 meatballs to the skillet, and brown on all sides for about 30 seconds to 1 minute per side. Transfer browned meatballs to the slow cooker, and repeat with remaining 1 tablespoon extra-virgin olive oil and meatballs.

7. Add white button mushrooms to the skillet, and sauté, stirring frequently, for 5 to 7 minutes or until browned. Transfer to the slow cooker.

8. Slice spaghetti squash in half from stem to blossom end. Scoop out seeds with a sturdy spoon, and gently place squash, rind side up, on top of meatballs in the slow cooker.

9. Cover and cook on high for 4 hours, on low for 6 to 8 hours, or until spaghetti squash is soft and meatballs are cooked through.

10. Carefully remove squash from the slow cooker, and use a metal fork to loosen and remove spaghetti-like strands. Top spaghetti squash with meatballs and sauce, and serve.

Chapter 9

Lamb Entrées

If you've never cooked lamb before, you'll be amazed how easy the slow cooker makes cooking this tender meat. The rich and meaty stews and braises in this chapter are deeply satisfying on a cold winter day, or you can spice up a special occasion with an impressive cut of lamb—and all feature the handy slow cooker, which does the majority of the kitchen work for you.

In this rich stew, sweetly spiced lamb is slow cooked with eggplant, mustard greens, and a hint of saffron.

Prep Time		Cook Time
20 minutes		3 to 8 hours
Yield		Serving Size
3 quarts (3 liters)		2 cups

Each serving has:

450 calories	15g carbohydrate	20g fat	54g protein

½ tsp. ground cardamom

½ tsp. ground cumin

2 tsp. sea salt

½ tsp. freshly ground black pepper

3 lb. (1.5kg) lamb shoulder, cut into 1-in. (2.5cm) pieces

2 TB. coconut oil

1 medium yellow onion, diced

2 cloves garlic, minced

6 cups beef broth

4 medium carrots, trimmed, peeled, and sliced

1 medium eggplant, trimmed and diced

1 lb. (450g) mustard greens, trimmed and chopped

1 (1-in.; 2.5cm) cinnamon stick

¼ tsp. saffron strands (optional)

½ cup fresh mint, chopped

1. In a large bowl, combine cardamom, cumin, sea salt, and black pepper.

2. Add lamb shoulder, and stir or toss until completely coated with spice mixture.

3. Heat a large skillet over medium-high heat. When hot, add 1 tablespoon coconut oil and wait 30 seconds. Add enough lamb cubes to cover the bottom of the pan, and cook, turning as needed, for 3 to 5 minutes or until browned. Transfer browned lamb to a 6- to 8-quart (5.5- to 7.5-liter) slow cooker. Repeat with remaining 1 tablespoon coconut oil and lamb.

4. Add yellow onion and garlic to the skillet, and sauté, stirring frequently, for 3 to 5 minutes or until onions are slightly translucent. Transfer onions and garlic to the slow cooker.

5. Pour ¼ cup beef broth into the pan, and use a wooden spoon to loosen browned bits. Add beef broth and browned bits to the slow cooker.

6. Add remaining 5¾ cups beef broth, carrots, eggplant, mustard greens, cinnamon stick, and saffron strands (if using) to the slow cooker.

7. Cover and cook on low for 6 to 8 hours, on high for 3 or 4 hours, or until lamb pieces are tender.

8. Top with fresh mint, and serve.

Saffron is a luxurious spice derived from the crocus flower. Because of the expense, it's optional in this recipe. If you do use it, it's helpful to place the strands in a 2-inch (5-centimeter) square of aluminum foil. Fold the foil into a packet, and place it in a dry, warm skillet for 1 or 2 minutes to release all the aromas before adding the saffron to the slow cooker.

Persian Lamb Stew

Braised Lamb Shoulder
with Rosemary and Garlic

This impressive dish is loaded with flavor. Lamb shoulder is slowly braised in beef broth with fresh rosemary and a generous helping of garlic.

Prep Time	Cook Time
10 minutes	5 to 10 hours
Yield	Serving Size
6 slices	2 slices

Each serving has:

795	1g	63g	53g
calories	carbohydrate	fat	protein

1 tsp. sea salt

½ tsp. freshly ground black pepper

4 lb. (2kg) lamb shoulder

2 TB. extra-virgin olive oil

2 cups beef broth

6 cloves garlic, crushed

6 sprigs fresh rosemary

1. In a small bowl, combine sea salt and black pepper. Rub seasonings on all sides of lamb shoulder.

2. Heat a medium skillet over medium-high heat. When hot, add extra-virgin olive oil and wait 30 seconds. Add lamb to the skillet, and cook for 3 to 5 minutes or until deeply browned. Turn over lamb, and brown on the other side. Transfer browned lamb to a 4- or 5-quart (4- to 5-liter) slow cooker.

3. Pour beef broth into the pan, and use a wooden spoon to loosen browned bits. Add broth and browned bits to the slow cooker.

4. Add garlic and rosemary to the slow cooker.

5. Cover and cook on low for 6 to 8 hours, on high for 3 or 4 hours, or until lamb reaches an internal temperature of 145°F (65°C) and is tender.

6. Transfer lamb to a cutting board, slice into 6 (1-inch; 2.5-centimeter) slices, and serve warm alongside steamed vegetables or with a green salad.

Six cloves of garlic might seem like a lot, but the strong flavor of lamb is perfectly suited to handle the garlic and the fresh rosemary.

Yellow turmeric pairs with ginger and cinnamon to add spice to lamb that's slow cooked with apricots, almonds, cauliflower, and a hint of lemon.

	Prep Time	Cook Time
	20 minutes	3 to 8 hours
	Yield	Serving Size
	3 quarts (3 liters)	2 cups

Each serving has:			
426 calories	25g carbohydrate	19g fat	38g protein

½ tsp. turmeric

½ tsp. ground ginger

¼ tsp. ground cinnamon

2 tsp. sea salt

½ tsp. freshly ground black pepper

2 lb. (1kg) lamb shoulder, cut into 1-in. (2.5cm) pieces

2 TB. coconut oil

1 medium yellow onion, diced

2 cloves garlic, minced

2 cups beef broth

1½ lb. (680g) cauliflower florets (about 1 large head)

1 cup dried apricots, halved

Zest of 1 medium lemon (about ½ tsp.)

½ cup slivered almonds

Juice of 1 medium lemon

½ cup fresh cilantro, chopped

1. In a medium bowl, combine turmeric, ginger, cinnamon, sea salt, and black pepper.

2. Add lamb shoulder, and stir or toss until completely coated with spice mixture.

3. Heat a large skillet over medium-high heat. When hot, add 1 tablespoon coconut oil and wait 30 seconds. Add enough lamb cubes to cover the bottom of the pan, and cook, turning as needed, for 3 to 5 minutes or until browned. Transfer to a 6- to 8-quart (5.5- to 7.5-liter) slow cooker, and repeat with remaining 1 tablespoon coconut oil and lamb cubes.

4. Add yellow onion and garlic to the skillet, and sauté, stirring frequently, for 3 to 5 minutes or until onions are slightly translucent. Transfer onions and garlic to the slow cooker.

5. Pour ¼ cup beef broth into the pan, and use a wooden spoon to loosen browned bits. Add beef broth and browned bits to the slow cooker.

6. Add remaining 1¾ cups beef broth, cauliflower, apricots, lemon zest, and slivered almonds to the slow cooker.

7. Cover and cook on low for 6 to 8 hours, on high for 3 or 4 hours, or until lamb pieces are tender.

8. Top with fresh lemon juice and cilantro, and serve.

A tagine is an earthenware pot with a flat base and a cone-shaped dome that returns cooking liquids to the cooking vessel. The return of condensation makes most tagine recipes well suited for slow cookers.

Lamb, Citrus, and Apricot Tagine

Coconut Lamb
with Cauliflower

These succulent lamb shanks, braised in tomato and coconut and served atop cauliflower, fall off the bone.

Prep Time	Cook Time
20 minutes	8 to 11 hours
Yield	Serving Size
4 shanks	½ shank

Each serving has:

527	15g	29g	52g
calories	carbohydrate	fat	protein

4 lb. (2kg) lamb shanks

2 TB. sea salt

1 TB. freshly ground black pepper

1 TB. coconut oil

1 medium yellow onion, diced

1 (28-oz.; 800g) can whole plum tomatoes, with juice

2 large carrots, trimmed, peeled, and sliced

1 (14-fl. oz.; 400ml) can full-fat coconut milk

1½ lb. (680g) cauliflower florets (about 1 large head)

½ cup fresh cilantro, chopped

1. Rub lamb shanks with sea salt and black pepper.

2. Heat a large skillet over medium-high heat. When hot, add coconut oil and wait 30 seconds. Add lamb shanks to the pan, and brown on all sides for about 30 seconds to 1 minute per side. Transfer lamb to a 6- to 8-quart (5.5- to 7.5-liter) slow cooker.

3. Add yellow onion to the pan, and sauté, stirring frequently, for 3 to 5 minutes or until slightly translucent. Transfer onions to the slow cooker.

4. Pour ¼ cup juice from plum tomatoes into the pan, and use a wooden spoon to loosen browned bits. Add tomato juice and browned bits to the slow cooker.

5. Add carrots, plum tomatoes with remaining juice, and coconut milk to the slow cooker.

6. Cover and cook on low for 6 to 8 hours.

7. Add cauliflower, cover, and cook for 2 or 3 hours or until lamb and vegetables are tender and cooked through.

8. Top with cilantro to serve.

Shanks are the toughest cut of lamb, which makes them perfectly suited for low and slow cooking times. If you can't find lamb shanks, you could use a leg or shoulder cut instead, but the cooking times might need to be adjusted. Just be sure the internal temperature reaches 145°F (65°C).

Thick zucchini noodles are slathered in a rich lamb sauce with tomatoes and Italian seasonings.

	Prep Time	Cook Time
	20 minutes	3 to 6 hours
	Yield	Serving Size
	8 cups	2 cups

Each serving has:

780 calories	19g carbohydrate	54g fat	42g protein

2 TB. extra-virgin olive oil

2 medium shallots, diced

1 clove garlic, minced

1 medium carrot, trimmed, peeled, and diced

½ cup red wine

2 lb. (1kg) ground lamb

1 (28-oz.; 800g) can diced tomatoes, with juice

1 TB. Italian blend seasoning

1 tsp. granulated garlic

¼ tsp. crushed red pepper flakes (optional)

1 bay leaf

2 tsp. sea salt

½ tsp. freshly ground black pepper

4 medium zucchini

1. Heat a large skillet over medium-high heat. When hot, add extra-virgin olive oil and wait 30 seconds. Add shallots, garlic, and carrot, and sauté, stirring frequently, for 3 to 5 minutes or until shallots are slightly translucent and carrots are softened. Transfer mixture to a 4- or 5-quart (4- to 5-liter) slow cooker.

2. Pour red wine into the pan, and use a wooden spoon to loosen browned bits. Pour red wine and browned bits into the slow cooker.

3. Add ground lamb to the slow cooker, and break apart with a wooden spoon.

4. Add tomatoes with juice, Italian blend seasoning, granulated garlic, crushed red pepper flakes (if using), bay leaf, sea salt, and black pepper.

5. Cover and cook on low for 5 or 6 hours or on high for 3 or 4 hours.

6. Meanwhile, using a vegetable peeler, peel zucchini lengthwise to create noodlelike ribbons. Refrigerate for later use.

7. Before serving, remove bay leaf and add zucchini ribbons. Stir with a wooden spoon to combine completely.

If you prefer, you can make this recipe with a 2-pound (1-kilogram) lamb shoulder. Brown the meat in a hot skillet with an additional 1 tablespoon extra-virgin olive oil for about 3 to 5 minutes, and shred the lamb shoulder just before adding the zucchini ribbons.

Lamb Ragout

Braised Leg of Lamb
with Fresh Mint Sauce

In this hearty dish, dark leg of lamb is slow-cooked with red wine, garlic, mushrooms, and parsnips and drizzled with a nutty, fresh mint sauce.

	Prep Time	Cook Time
	20 minutes	4 to 8 hours
	Yield	Serving Size
	20 slices	2 slices

Each serving has:

659	27g	27g	44g
calories	carbohydrate	fat	protein

2¼ tsp. sea salt

¾ tsp. freshly ground black pepper

5 lb. (2.5kg) boneless leg of lamb

3 TB. extra-virgin olive oil

1 cup red wine

2 cups beef broth

3 cloves garlic, crushed

1 lb. (450g) small white or brown mushrooms

3 lb. (1.5kg) parsnips, peeled and sliced

2 cups fresh mint leaves, minced

½ cup slivered almonds

1 tsp. grade B maple syrup

3 TB. white wine vinegar

1. In a small bowl, combine 2 teaspoons sea salt and ½ teaspoon black pepper. Rub mixture on all sides of leg of lamb.

2. Heat a medium skillet over medium-high heat. When hot, add 1 tablespoon extra-virgin olive oil and wait 30 seconds. Add lamb to the skillet, and cook for 3 to 5 minutes or until deeply browned. Turn and brown on the other side. Transfer lamb to a 6- to 8-quart (5.5- to 7.5-liter) slow cooker.

3. Pour red wine into the pan, and use a wooden spoon to loosen browned bits. Add red wine and browned bits to the slow cooker.

4. Add beef broth, garlic, mushrooms, and parsnips to the slow cooker.

5. Cover and cook on low for 6 to 8 hours, on high for 4 or 5 hours, or until lamb reaches an internal temperature of 145°F (65°C).

6. Meanwhile, in a blender or a small food processor fitted with a chopping blade, pulse remaining ¼ teaspoon sea salt, remaining ¼ teaspoon black pepper, remaining 2 tablespoons extra-virgin olive oil, mint, almonds, maple syrup, and white wine vinegar for 15 to 25 seconds to form sauce.

7. Transfer lamb to a cutting board, slice into 20 (½-inch; 1-centimeter) slices, and serve over parsnips, drizzled with fresh mint sauce.

If you have a slow cooker that will hold it, you can use a bone-in leg of lamb instead. Just increase the cooking time by about 1 hour.

Chapter 10

Seafood Suppers

Seafood doesn't naturally lend itself to slow cooking. However, you'll find the allure of a slow cooked broth with a handful of fresh seafood gently coaxed to perfection by its warmth hard to resist. Try a few of these recipes, and you'll soon find that they are easy and delicious.

Seasoned to perfection, this tasty fish broth adds flavor to any fish-based recipe.

Prep Time	Cook Time
10 minutes	8 to 24 hours

Yield	Serving Size
4 quarts (4 liters)	2 cups

Each serving has:

79 calories	2g carbohydrate	3g fat	10g protein

1 large fish head

1 lb. (450g) bones from halibut, bass, cod, or other whitefish

3 large leeks, sliced

2 medium carrots, sliced

3 to 5 sprigs fresh thyme

1 cup fresh parsley, chopped

1 TB. sea salt

1 tsp. whole black peppercorns

1 bay leaf

½ cup dry white wine

5 qt. (4.75l) water

1. In a 6- to 8-quart (5.5- to 7.5-liter) slow cooker, combine fish head, fish bones, leeks, carrots, thyme, parsley, sea salt, black peppercorns, bay leaf, white wine, and water.

2. Cover and cook on low for 6 to 24 hours, occasionally skimming off and discarding any white foam off top of broth.

3. Strain through a fine sieve to separate fish bones and vegetables from broth. Discard vegetables and bones.

4. Use broth immediately as a base for soups or stews, or freeze in portions for later use.

If you can't find a fish head—or don't like the look of it—you can use 2 pounds (1 kilogram) bones instead.

Fish Broth

Salmon Chowder

Puréed leeks and celery root make a creamy base for this rich, nondairy chowder accented with smoked salmon pieces, a sprinkling of fresh dill, and a bit of kick from the seasonings.

Prep Time	Cook Time
25 minutes	6 to 8 hours

Yield	Serving Size
3 quarts (3 liters)	2 cups

Each serving has:

285 calories	37g carbohydrate	8g fat	17g protein

2 TB. extra-virgin olive oil

8 cups sliced leeks, white and light green parts only (about 6 large leeks)

½ cup dry white wine

3 lb. (1.5kg) celery root or celeriac, trimmed, peeled, and diced

1 large carrot, trimmed, peeled, and diced

3 cloves garlic, minced

8 cups vegetable stock

2 TB. Old Bay seafood seasoning

2 tsp. sea salt

1 tsp. freshly ground black pepper

2 bay leaves

Juice of 1 medium lemon

¾ lb. (340g) smoked salmon, flaked into small pieces

½ cup fresh dill, chopped

1. Heat a medium skillet over medium-high heat. When hot, add extra-virgin olive oil and wait 30 seconds. Add leeks to the pan, and sauté, stirring frequently, for 3 to 5 minutes or until slightly translucent. Transfer leeks to a 6- to 8-quart (5.5- to 7.5-liter) slow cooker.

2. Pour white wine into the pan, and use a wooden spoon to loosen browned bits. Pour white wine and browned bits into the slow cooker.

3. Add celery root, carrot, garlic, vegetable stock, Old Bay seafood seasoning, sea salt, black pepper, and bay leaves to the slow cooker, and stir with a wooden spoon to combine.

4. Cover and cook on high for 6 to 8 hours or until vegetables are tender.

5. Remove and discard bay leaves. Using an immersion blender, purée soup in the slow cooker.

6. Add lemon juice and smoked salmon, and stir with a wooden spoon. Taste and adjust seasonings if needed.

7. Top with fresh dill to serve.

If you can't find Old Bay seafood seasoning, you can make your own by combining equal parts celery salt, freshly ground black pepper, and paprika, along with a dash of cayenne.

Ground pork sausage, cayenne, and fire-roasted tomatoes add Cajun flair to this slow cooked fish stew.

Prep Time	Cook Time
15 minutes	3 to 5 hours
Yield	Serving Size
8 cups	2 cups

Each serving has:

452	17g	25g	37g
calories	carbohydrate	fat	protein

2 TB. extra-virgin olive oil

1 medium yellow onion, diced

2 cloves garlic, minced

½ lb. (225g) ground pork sausage

1 large celery stalk, diced

1 large carrot, peeled, trimmed, and diced

1 bay leaf

½ tsp. cayenne

1 (28-oz.; 800g) can fire-roasted, crushed tomatoes, with juice

1 medium red bell pepper, ribs and seeds removed, and diced

5 cups fish broth

1 lb. (450g) firm, skinless whitefish fillets, sliced

1 tsp. sea salt

¼ tsp. freshly ground black pepper

Juice of 2 medium lemons

1. Heat a large skillet over medium-high heat. When hot, add extra-virgin olive oil and wait 30 seconds. Add yellow onion and garlic to the pan, and sauté, stirring frequently, for 3 to 5 minutes or until onions are slightly translucent.

2. Add pork sausage to the pan, and cook for 3 to 5 minutes. Transfer contents of skillet to a 4- or 5-quart (4- to 5-liter) slow cooker.

3. Add celery, carrot, bay leaf, cayenne, fire-roasted tomatoes with juice, red bell pepper, and fish broth to the slow cooker, and stir with a wooden spoon to combine.

4. Cover and cook on low for 4 or 5 hours, on high for 3 or 4 hours, or until vegetables are tender.

5. Meanwhile, season whitefish with sea salt and black pepper. Refrigerate for later use.

6. 5 minutes before serving, remove bay leaf.

7. Add whitefish and lemon juice, stir gently, and cook for 5 minutes or until fish is completely cooked.

8. Adjust seasonings, if desired, and serve hot.

For a little extra flavor, feel free to add 1 tablespoon of your favorite Cajun seasoning blend. Just be sure the spice blend you use doesn't contain any additional sugar or non-Paleo ingredients.

Creole Fish Stew

Cioppino

This tomato-based seafood stew gets its complex flavor from a blend of Italian spices, a splash of white wine, and the zip of crushed red pepper flakes.

Prep Time	Cook Time
15 minutes	6 to 8 hours
Yield	Serving Size
3 quarts (3 liters)	2 cups

Each serving has:

374 calories	12g carbohydrate	11g fat	49g protein

3 TB. extra-virgin olive oil

1 medium yellow onion, diced

3 cloves garlic, minced

1 cup dry white wine

4 cups fish broth

2 TB. tomato paste

1 (28-oz.; 800g) can diced tomatoes, with juice

½ tsp. crushed red pepper flakes

1 tsp. Italian seasoning blend

1 bay leaf

2 TB. sea salt

1 TB. freshly ground black pepper

1 lb. (450g) fresh mussels or manila clams (optional)

1 lb. (450g) raw shrimp, peeled and deveined

½ lb. (225g) raw calamari (optional)

1 lb. (450g) firm, boneless whitefish fillets, sliced

½ cup fresh parsley, chopped

1. Heat a medium skillet over medium-high heat. When hot, add extra-virgin olive oil and wait 30 seconds. Add yellow onion and garlic to the pan, and sauté, stirring frequently, for 3 to 5 minutes or until onions are slightly translucent. Transfer onions and garlic to a 6- to 8-quart (5.5- to 7.5-liter) slow cooker.

2. Pour ¼ cup white wine into the pan, and use a wooden spoon to loosen browned bits. Add white wine and browned bits to the slow cooker.

3. Add remaining ¾ cup white wine, fish broth, tomato paste, diced tomatoes with juice, crushed red pepper flakes, Italian seasoning blend, bay leaf, sea salt, and black pepper to the slow cooker, and stir.

4. Cover and cook on low for 6 to 8 hours.

5. 5 minutes before serving, remove bay leaf. Add mussels (if using), and cook for 2 minutes.

6. Add shrimp, calamari (if using), and whitefish, and stir.

7. Discard any mussels or clams that did not open. Season with additional sea salt if desired, and serve topped with fresh parsley.

A note on fresh seafood: always get fresh seafood from a reputable and responsible source. This dish is traditionally served with fresh mussels or clams, but feel free to skip them if you can't find a good supply.

Light and flaky whitefish is slow cooked with cabbage, cauliflower, and carrots in a zesty curry.

Prep Time	Cook Time
15 minutes	3 to 5 hours
Yield	Serving Size
8 cups	2 cups

Each serving has:

340 calories	28g carbohydrate	12g fat	37g protein

2 TB. extra-virgin olive oil

1 medium yellow onion, diced

2 cloves garlic, minced

2 cups fish broth

1 TB. curry powder

½ tsp. cayenne (optional)

1½ lb. (680g) cauliflower florets (about 1 large head)

2 medium carrots, trimmed, peeled, and sliced

1 small head green cabbage, thinly sliced

1 lb. (450g) skinless sea bass fillets, sliced

1 tsp. sea salt

¼ tsp. freshly ground black pepper

1. Heat a medium skillet over medium-high heat. When hot, add extra-virgin olive oil and wait 30 seconds. Add yellow onion and garlic to the pan, and sauté, stirring frequently, for 3 to 5 minutes or until onions are slightly translucent. Transfer onions and garlic to a 4- or 5-quart (4- to 5-liter) slow cooker.

2. Pour ¼ cup fish broth into the pan, and use a wooden spoon to loosen browned bits. Add fish broth and browned bits to the slow cooker.

3. Add remaining 1¾ cups fish broth, curry powder, cayenne (optional), cauliflower, carrots, and green cabbage to the slow cooker, and stir with a wooden spoon to combine.

4. Cover and cook on low for 4 or 5 hours, on high for 3 or 4 hours, or until vegetables are tender.

5. Meanwhile, season sea bass with sea salt and black pepper. Refrigerate for later use.

6. 5 minutes before serving, add sea bass to the slow cooker, and stir gently.

7. Adjust seasonings, if desired, and serve hot.

This recipe is also great with shrimp. Toss 1 pound (450 grams) raw, peeled shrimp in instead of, or at the same time as, the sea bass.

Curried Vegetables
with Sea Bass

Shrimp Tikka Masala

Pungent curry and fresh ginger add zip to cauliflower in this rich dish. Cooled with creamy coconut milk and topped with shrimp, this no-fuss meal is loaded with flavor.

Prep Time	Cook Time
20 minutes	3 to 6 hours
Yield	Serving Size
8 cups	2 cups

Each serving has:

449	23g	26g	31g
calories	carbohydrate	fat	protein

2 TB. coconut oil, melted

2 tsp. sea salt

½ tsp. freshly ground black pepper

1 TB. paprika

1 TB. garam masala

1 TB. curry powder

¼ tsp. cayenne (optional)

1½ lb. (680g) cauliflower florets (about 1 large head)

1 (14-fl. oz.; 400ml) can full-fat coconut milk

¼ cup tomato paste

1 (15-oz.; 420g) can diced tomatoes, with juice

4 cloves garlic, minced

1 (1-in.; 2.5cm) fresh gingerroot, peeled and grated

1 lb. (450g) fresh shrimp, peeled

½ cup fresh cilantro, chopped

1. In a medium bowl, combine coconut oil, sea salt, black pepper, paprika, garam masala, curry powder, and cayenne (if using).

2. Add cauliflower, and toss to completely coat in spice mixture. Transfer cauliflower to a 6- to 8-quart (5.5- to 7.5-liter) slow cooker.

3. Add coconut milk, tomato paste, diced tomatoes with juice, garlic, and gingerroot to the slow cooker, and stir with a wooden spoon.

4. Cover and cook on low for 4 to 6 hours, on high for 3 or 4 hours, or until cauliflower is tender.

5. Add shrimp.

6. Cover and cook for 10 to 15 minutes or until shrimp are bright pink and cooked through.

7. Taste, season with sea salt, top with fresh cilantro, and serve.

Curry powder comes in many different versions. This recipe calls for two different kinds—curry powder and garam masala—to give the shrimp a greater depth of flavor. You could substitute 2 tablespoons of one if that's all you can find or have on hand.

Chapter 11

On the Side

If you're looking for the perfect vegetable to serve alongside a protein-packed meal, this is the chapter for you. The sensational side recipes that follow often feature faster cook times in the slow cooker and enable you to use your oven for the main course. These excellent sides also allow you to focus on something else and still get your side-dish vegetables cooked to perfection.

Collard Greens

These collards have a kick! Crushed red pepper flakes and salty pancetta are slow cooked to perfection with tender collard greens.

Prep Time	Cook Time
15 minutes	2 or 3 hours
Yield	Serving Size
4 cups	1 cup

Each serving has:

93 calories	16g carbohydrate	9g fat	6g protein

1 TB. extra-virgin olive or coconut oil

1 small shallot, diced

1 oz. (25g) pancetta, diced (about ½ cup)

¼ cup chicken stock

1 lb. (450g) collard greens, stems removed and roughly chopped

¼ tsp. sea salt

¼ tsp. crushed red pepper flakes

1. Heat a small skillet over medium-high heat. When hot, add extra-virgin olive oil and wait 30 seconds. Add shallot, and sauté, stirring frequently, for 30 seconds to 1 minute or until slightly translucent.

2. Add pancetta, and cook, stirring occasionally, for 1 or 2 minutes or until meat begins to brown. Transfer shallot and pancetta to a 4- or 5-quart (4- to 5-liter) slow cooker.

3. Add chicken stock to the skillet, and use a wooden spoon to loosen browned bits. Add chicken stock and browned bits to the slow cooker

4. Add collard greens, sea salt, and crushed red pepper flakes to the slow cooker, and stir to coat.

5. Cover and cook on low for 2 or 3 hours or until greens are tender.

6. Serve hot.

You can use any sturdy green such as kale or mustard greens in place of the collards. Curly varieties of kale will hold on to the pancetta and pepper flakes and be extra tasty.

The slow cooker is the perfect tool for creating these sweet and simple onions.

	Prep Time		Cook Time
	15 minutes		10 to 14 hours
	Yield		Serving Size
	4 cups		½ cup

Each serving has:			
99	0g	3g	0g
calories	carbohydrate	fat	protein

3 lb. (1.5kg) sweet yellow onions

2 TB. extra-virgin olive oil

½ tsp. sea salt

¼ tsp. freshly ground black pepper

1. Slice sweet yellow onions into ¼-inch (.5-centimeter) rings.

2. Place onions, extra-virgin olive oil, sea salt, and black pepper in a 4- or 5-quart (4- to 5-liter) slow cooker, and stir to coat onions with oil and seasoning.

3. Cover and cook on low for 10 to 14 hours or until onions are soft and caramelized.

4. Serve hot.

Use these onions as a topping for grilled steaks or pork chops, or as an excellent addition to hearty kale salads with balsamic vinegar. Use the leftover cooking juices to add slow cooked flavor to quick soups. Freeze leftovers in small portions for later use.

Caramelized Onions

Mushroom Ragout

A woodsy blend of mushrooms are slow cooked in wine and grassy herbs until they're creamy and rich.

Prep Time	Cook Time
15 minutes	8 to 10 hours
Yield	Serving Size
4 cups	1 cup

Each serving has:

144	16g	0g	11g
calories	carbohydrate	fat	protein

2 TB. extra-virgin olive oil

1 medium shallot, diced

1 cup dry cooking wine or vegetable broth

1 lb. (450g) white button mushrooms, sliced

1 lb. (450g) portobello mushrooms, sliced

1 lb. (450g) crimini or chanterelle mushrooms, sliced

½ tsp. sea salt

¼ tsp. freshly ground black pepper

½ tsp. dried thyme

¼ cup fresh parsley, chopped

1. Heat a medium skillet over medium-high heat. When hot, add extra-virgin olive oil and wait 30 seconds. Add shallot, and sauté, stirring frequently, for 1 or 2 minutes or until slightly browned and translucent. Transfer shallot to a 4- or 5-quart (4- to 5-liter) slow cooker.

2. Add cooking wine, white button mushrooms, portobello mushrooms, crimini mushrooms, sea salt, black pepper, and thyme to the slow cooker, and stir to combine.

3. Cover and cook on low for 8 to 10 hours or until mushrooms are soft.

4. Sprinkle with fresh parsley to serve.

If you prefer a creamier ragout, substitute 1 cup full-fat coconut milk for the dry wine or vegetable broth.

This simple dish is nice alongside any main dish recipe in the book. And it's easy: add the parchment packet, cover, cook, and return to perfectly cooked green beans steamed with rosemary and thyme.

Prep Time	Cook Time
15 minutes	20 to 30 minutes
Yield	Serving Size
4 cups	1 cup

	Each serving has:		
64 calories	8g carbohydrate	4g fat	2g protein

1 lb. (450g) fresh green beans, trimmed

1 sprig fresh rosemary

1 sprig fresh thyme

1 TB. coconut oil

¼ tsp. sea salt

Dash freshly ground black pepper

1. Cut a 24-inch (60-centimeter) length of parchment paper.

2. Rinse and drain green beans, but do not dry them. Place wet green beans, rosemary, and thyme in the center of the parchment paper. Fold over paper several times to create a packet around beans.

3. Place the packet on top of the slow cooker meal you're cooking, cover, and cook for 15 to 30 minutes or until green beans are as tender as you like them.

4. Carefully remove the packet from the slow cooker, and unwrap—a lot of steam will escape as you open it. Transfer contents to a medium bowl.

5. Remove and discard rosemary and thyme sprigs.

6. Add coconut oil, sea salt, and black pepper, and stir until coconut oil melts and coats beans.

7. Serve warm alongside your main dish.

Variation: For **Asparagus with Fresh Herbs,** substitute 1 pound (450 grams) fresh, trimmed asparagus spears instead for the green beans, and use tarragon instead of rosemary. You might need to cut a larger piece of parchment paper or cross two pieces to form an X and place the vegetables in the center, tied securely with cooking twine.

This recipe works well with roast meats and braises, but it isn't the best for soups and stews. The excessive liquid could seep into the parchment packet if it isn't wrapped tight enough.

Green Beans
with Fresh Herbs

Garlic-Mashed Cauliflower

If you miss garlic-mashed potatoes, these Paleo-friendly mashed cauliflower florets with silky coconut, garlic, and fresh herbs might just make you forget about spuds.

Prep Time	Cook Time
15 minutes	3 or 4 hours
Yield	Serving Size
4 cups	1 cup

Each serving has:

115	13g	6g	4g
calories	carbohydrate	fat	protein

1½ lb. (680g) cauliflower florets (about 1 large head)

2 cloves garlic, crushed

1 TB. fresh rosemary, chopped

½ cup full-fat coconut milk

½ tsp. sea salt

¼ tsp. freshly ground black pepper

1. In a 4- or 5-quart (4- to 5-liter) slow cooker, combine cauliflower, garlic, rosemary, coconut milk, sea salt, and black pepper with a wooden spoon.

2. Cover and cook on high for 3 or 4 hours or until cauliflower is tender.

3. Use an immersion blender to purée cauliflower into a smooth paste.

4. Season with additional sea salt, and serve warm.

For a summery version, replace the rosemary with 3 or 4 chopped fresh chives, and add 1 teaspoon lemon pepper seasoning.

Smoky chipotle and toasty almonds will make this easy spaghetti squash side an instant favorite.

Prep Time	Cook Time
5 minutes	2 to 6 hours
Yield	Serving Size
4 cups	1 cup

Each serving has:

141	3g	9g	4g
calories	carbohydrate	fat	protein

3 lb. (1.5kg) spaghetti squash

1 cup water

1 tsp. coconut oil

1 tsp. ground chipotle

1 tsp. sea salt

½ cup slivered almonds, toasted

1. Using a heavy knife, slice spaghetti squash in half from stem to blossom end. Scoop out and discard seeds.

2. Place squash halves rind side down in a 6- to 8-quart (5.5- to 7.5-liter) slow cooker. Pour water around squash.

3. Cover and cook on high for 2 or 3 hours, on low for 4 to 6 hours, or until squash is tender to the touch.

4. Carefully remove squash from the slow cooker, and use a metal fork to loosen and remove spaghetti-like strands of squash into a large bowl.

5. Add coconut oil, chipotle, and sea salt, and stir to combine.

6. Top with almonds, and serve.

Be sure to pull the squash strands out crosswise instead of lengthwise. If you're not sure which is the right direction, try both and go with the one that makes it look like spaghetti!

Spicy Spaghetti Squash

Brussels Sprouts
with Hazelnuts and Pancetta

Salty pancetta and crisped shallots dress these brussels sprouts. A topping of hazelnuts offers a satisfying crunch.

Prep Time	Cook Time
15 minutes	2 or 3 hours
Yield	Serving Size
6 cups	1½ cups

Each serving has:

188 calories	20g carbohydrate	14g fat	9g protein

1 TB. extra-virgin olive oil

2 oz. (55g) shallot, diced (about 1 small shallot)

1 oz. (25g) pancetta, diced (about ½ cup)

¼ cup chicken stock

1 lb. (450g) brussels sprouts, trimmed and halved

¼ tsp. sea salt (optional)

½ cup roasted hazelnuts, chopped

1. Heat a small skillet over medium-high heat. When hot, add extra-virgin olive oil and wait 30 seconds. Add shallot, and sauté, stirring frequently, for 30 seconds to 1 minute or until slightly translucent.

2. Add pancetta, and cook, stirring occasionally, for 1 or 2 minutes or until meat begins to brown. Transfer shallot and pancetta to a 4- or 5-quart (4- to 5-liter) slow cooker.

3. Add chicken stock to the skillet, and use a wooden spoon to loosen browned bits. Add chicken stock and browned bits to the slow cooker.

4. Add brussels sprouts to the slow cooker, and stir to coat.

5. Cover and cook on low for 2 or 3 hours or until brussels sprouts are tender.

6. Season with sea salt (if using), top with hazelnuts, and serve.

Like bacon or ham, pancetta does contain a small amount of sugar due to the brining process. If you'd prefer to skip all sugars, you could use a finely chopped 2-ounce (55-gram) boneless, skinless chicken thigh seasoned with ½ teaspoon sea salt instead.

Earthy beets, sweet pearl onions, and briny olives blend together with fresh mint for a truly unique side dish.

Prep Time	Cook Time
15 minutes	2 or 3 hours
Yield	Serving Size
6 cups	1 cup

Each serving has:

136	19g	6g	3g
calories	carbohydrate	fat	protein

2 lb. (1kg) beets, trimmed, peeled, and sliced

16 pearl onions, trimmed, peeled, and halved

½ cup black olives

2 tsp. extra-virgin olive oil

½ tsp. sea salt

¼ tsp. freshly ground black pepper

¼ cup fresh mint, chopped

1. In a 4- or 5-quart (4- to 5-liter) slow cooker, combine beets, pearl onions, black olives, extra-virgin olive oil, sea salt, and black pepper with a wooden spoon to coat beets and onions with oil and seasoning.

2. Cover and cook on low for 2 or 3 hours or until beets are tender.

3. Sprinkle with fresh mint, and serve.

This side can be served as a warm side or a cold salad, depending upon the season. You can also use golden beets and green olives for a lighter, sweeter, summertime variation.

Braised Beets
with Pearl Onions, Olives, and Mint

Chapter 12

Paleo-Friendly Desserts

Just because you don't eat sugar doesn't mean you have to miss out on sweets. The decadent Paleo desserts in this chapter are a real treat for when you're feeling deprived of sugar. Keep in mind that if you're trying to lose weight, you still should be mindful of the portion size and how often you indulge in these carbohydrate-rich treats.

Stewed Peaches

Honey-sweetened peaches are cooked in citrus with a hint of cinnamon in this fruit-based dessert.

Prep Time	Cook Time
5 minutes	4 to 6 hours
Yield	Serving Size
4 cups	½ cup

Each serving has:

139 calories	51g carbohydrate	4g fat	0g protein

3 (15-oz.; 420g) cans sliced peaches in juice, drained

2 TB. coconut oil

⅓ cup raw honey

Juice of 1 medium lemon

½ cup unsweetened orange juice (about 1 medium orange)

1 tsp. ground cinnamon

1. In a 3- or 4- quart (3- to 4-liter) slow cooker, combine peaches, coconut oil, honey, lemon juice, orange juice, and cinnamon to coat peaches.

2. Cover and cook on low for 4 to 6 hours or until peaches begin to break down. Turn off the slow cooker.

3. Using an immersion blender, break down peaches into a coarse sauce. Or leave in slices if you prefer.

4. Serve warm or chilled.

Variation: To make **Habanero Stewed Peaches,** add 1 habanero pepper, slit three times with a sharp knife. Remove the pepper before serving or storing peaches.

These peaches are excellent on their own, or you can use them as a coconut ice cream topping or a jam for Paleo muffins or bread.

In this warming dessert, stewed apples are infused with cinnamon and nutmeg, with a crunchy, crumbly, honey-sweet topping.

Prep Time	Cook Time
20 minutes	4 to 8 hours
Yield	Serving Size
10 slices	1 slice

Each serving has:

278	26g	19g	4g
calories	carbohydrate	fat	protein

½ cup unsweetened orange juice (about 1 medium orange)

2 lb. (1kg) apples (about 7 medium apples)

1 TB. loose-packed lemon zest (about 1 medium lemon)

3 TB. raw honey

½ tsp. freshly grated nutmeg

1¼ tsp. ground cinnamon (¼ tsp. optional)

3 TB. coconut oil, melted

¾ cup unsweetened shredded coconut

¾ cup almond flour

¾ cup walnuts or pecans, chopped

¼ tsp. sea salt

1. Pour orange juice into a 6- to 8-quart (5.5- to 7.5-liter) slow cooker.

2. Peel, core, and thinly slice each apple and immediately immerse in orange juice to keep them from turning brown while you prepare remaining apples.

3. Add lemon zest, 1 tablespoon honey, nutmeg, and 1 teaspoon cinnamon to the slow cooker, and use a wooden spoon to combine.

4. Cover and cook on low for 6 to 8 hours or on high for 4 to 6 hours.

5. Meanwhile, in a medium bowl, combine remaining 2 tablespoons honey, coconut oil, shredded coconut, almond flour, walnuts, and sea salt until a crumbly mixture forms. Refrigerate for later use.

6. 1 hour before serving, spread crumble mixture over apples in the slow cooker. Lightly sprinkle with remaining ¼ teaspoon cinnamon (if using).

7. Cover, but use a wooden spoon to keep the lid propped open, and cook for 1 hour.

8. Serve warm on its own or with a scoop of coconut ice cream.

It's almost impossible to overcook the apples in this recipe. For a hassle-free dessert, prepare and refrigerate the sliced apples before bed one night, place them in the slow cooker and turn it on before you leave for work the next day, and add the crisp topping when you get home.

Apple Crisp

Mixed Berry Cobbler
with Coconut Whipped Cream

Warm berries and crumbly cake pair perfectly with sweet coconut cream in this classic dessert.

Prep Time
15 minutes

Cook Time
3 hours

Yield
10 slices

Serving Size
1 slice

Each serving has:

341
calories

24g
carbohydrate

25g
fat

9g
protein

2 cups almond flour

¼ cup coconut flour

1 tsp. baking powder

¼ tsp. sea salt

3 large eggs, whisked

6 TB. raw honey

¾ cup full-fat coconut milk

1 tsp. pure vanilla extract

1 tsp. ground cinnamon

1 lb. (450g) frozen mixed berries

1 (14-fl. oz.; 400ml) can coconut cream

1. Line a 6- to 8-quart (5.5- to 7.5-liter) slow cooker with two pieces of parchment paper.

2. In a large bowl, combine almond flour, coconut flour, baking powder, and sea salt using a metal fork. Set aside.

3. In a medium bowl, whisk together eggs, 4 tablespoons honey, coconut milk, vanilla extract, and cinnamon. Pour egg mixture into dry ingredients, and combine completely. Pour batter into the slow cooker.

4. Add mixed berries to the slow cooker, and use a butter knife to swirl berries into batter.

5. Cover, but use a wooden spoon to keep the lid propped open, and cook on low for 2½ hours or until set.

6. Remove the lid completely, turn off the slow cooker, and let rest for 30 minutes.

7. Just before serving, in a small bowl, whisk together remaining 2 tablespoons honey and coconut cream.

8. Top warm cobbler with coconut cream, and serve.

Variation: For **Peach Cobbler with Coconut Whipped Cream,** replace the mixed berries with 1 pound (450 grams) frozen sliced peaches.

Because of all the fruit, this cobbler is best served the day you make it. Although it will still be tasty, it can get a little soggy if it's refrigerated overnight.

Creamy coconut meets mouth-puckering lemon in this quick-and-easy recipe. Chia seeds add an extra pop as well as a powerful blood sugar stabilizer to balance out the honey.

Prep Time	Cook Time
15 minutes	1 hour, plus 1 hour chill time
Yield	Serving Size
2 cups	½ cup

Each serving has:			
320 calories	16g carbohydrate	25g fat	6g protein

1 (14-fl. oz.; 400ml) can full-fat coconut milk

1 TB. loose-packed lemon zest (about 1 medium lemon)

¼ cup lemon juice (about 2 medium lemons)

2 TB. raw honey

⅛ tsp. sea salt

6 TB. chia seeds

1. In a 2- or 3-quart (2- to 3-liter) slow cooker, combine coconut milk, lemon zest, lemon juice, honey, sea salt, and chia seeds.

2. Cover and cook on low for 1 hour.

3. Remove pudding from the slow cooker, and refrigerate for at least 1 hour.

4. Serve chilled.

Variation: To make **Lemon and Berry Parfaits,** layer Lemon Chia Pudding into a tall glass with ½ cup fresh blackberries and ½ cup sliced fresh strawberries.

For a sweeter and less acidic-tasting treat, use Meyer lemons.

Lemon Chia Pudding

Raspberry Almond Cake

Tart raspberries are the perfect complement to the toasty warm flavor of almonds in this aromatic bundtlike cake.

Prep Time	Cook Time
15 minutes	3 hours
Yield	Serving Size
10 slices	1 slice

Each serving has:

352	18g	29g	12g
calories	carbohydrate	fat	protein

1 cup almond flour

¼ cup coconut flour

½ tsp. baking soda

½ tsp. baking powder

¼ tsp. sea salt

3 large eggs, whisked

1 cup almond butter, at room temperature

¼ cup raw honey

¼ cup coconut oil, melted

½ tsp. pure almond extract

⅓ cup slivered almonds

¾ cup fresh raspberries

1. Lightly grease the inside of a 6- to 8-quart (5.5- to 7.5-liter) slow cooker, about 2 inches (5 centimeters) up the sides, with coconut oil. Cut a piece of parchment paper to fit snugly in the bottom of the crock. Grease the sides of an ovenproof soufflé dish about 4 inches (10 centimeters) in diameter, and invert in the center of the crock.

2. In a medium bowl, combine almond flour, coconut flour, baking soda, baking powder, and sea salt using a metal fork.

3. In a large bowl, and using a heavy whisk or an electric mixer on medium speed, combine eggs, almond butter, honey, coconut oil, and almond extract.

4. Add dry ingredients to wet ingredients, and combine completely.

5. Carefully fold in almonds and raspberries, and pour batter into the prepared slow cooker.

6. Cover, but use a wooden spoon to keep the lid propped open, and cook on low for 2½ hours.

7. Remove the lid completely, turn off the slow cooker, and let rest for 30 minutes.

8. Invert a plate large enough to hold cake and small enough to fit inside the slow cooker, and place it on top of cake. Keeping the plate in place, carefully invert the crock to remove cake.

9. Remove the parchment paper, and cool cake completely before slicing and serving.

To allow the cake to cook through, it must be made in a larger slow cooker. Be sure the batter isn't more than 2 inches (5 centimeters) thick to get the best results.

These brownies have a hint of lemon and extra dark chocolate. They're so decadent!

Prep Time		Cook Time	
15 minutes		2 hours	
Yield		Serving Size	
10 slices		1 slice	

Each serving has:

197	19g	13g	7g
calories	carbohydrate	fat	protein

2 TB. coconut flour

¼ tsp. sea salt

¾ tsp. baking powder

¼ cup unsweetened cocoa powder

3 large eggs, whisked

½ cup almond butter, at room temperature

½ cup raw honey

½ tsp. pure vanilla extract

1 tsp. lemon zest

½ cup dark chocolate chips (at least 75 percent cacao)

½ cup raw walnuts or pecans, chopped (optional)

1. Line a 6- to 8-quart (5.5- to 7.5-liter) slow cooker with parchment paper.

2. In a medium bowl, combine coconut flour, sea salt, baking powder, and cocoa powder using a metal fork.

3. In a large bowl, and using a heavy whisk or an electric mixer on medium speed, combine eggs, almond butter, honey, vanilla extract, and lemon zest.

4. Add dry ingredients to wet ingredients, and combine completely.

5. Fold in dark chocolate chips and walnuts (if using), and pour batter into the prepared slow cooker.

6. Cover, but use a wooden spoon to keep the lid propped open, and cook on low for 1½ to 2 hours or until a knife inserted into the middle comes out clean.

7. Remove the lid completely, turn off the slow cooker, and let rest for 15 minutes before slicing and serving.

Add an extra handful of dark chocolate chips if you want extra-gooey, extra-chocolaty brownies.

Paleo Brownies

Dark Chocolate Sauce

Decadent dark chocolate is melted with coconut cream and a hint of honey to make this truly indulgent treat. Eat it on its own, as a dip for fresh fruit slices or berries, or as a rich frosting.

Prep Time	Cook Time
5 minutes	1 hour
Yield	Serving Size
2 cups	¼ cup

Each serving has:

236	8g	23g	4g
calories	carbohydrate	fat	protein

7 oz. (200g) 100 percent cacao unsweetened chocolate bars

1 (14-fl. oz.; 400ml) can coconut cream

1 or 2 TB. raw honey

⅛ tsp. sea salt

1. Break chocolate bars into small chunks. Set aside.

2. In a 2- or 3-quart (2- to 3-liter) slow cooker, whisk together coconut cream, honey, and sea salt.

3. Add chocolate pieces.

4. Cover and cook on low for 1 hour or until chocolate melts entirely.

5. Whisk mixture again to fully incorporate melted chocolate, and serve warm.

Variation: To make **Mexican Chocolate Sauce,** add ½ teaspoon cayenne. To make **Paleo Chocolate Hazelnut Spread,** add ½ cup hazelnut butter.

This dessert is what slow cookers were made for. Double or triple the recipe for a large gathering, but be sure to stir every hour to prevent the chocolate from scorching.

Maple-glazed yams are slow cooked in fresh orange juice and cloves and topped with crunchy pecans.

Prep Time	Cook Time
15 minutes	2½ to 3 hours
Yield	Serving Size
4 cups	½ cup

Each serving has:

264 calories	39g carbohydrate	12g fat	3g protein

3 lb. (1.5kg) yams, peeled

¼ tsp. sea salt

½ tsp. ground cloves

2 TB. coconut oil, melted

⅓ cup grade B maple syrup

½ cup unsweetened orange juice (about 1 medium orange)

¾ cup pecans, chopped

1. Using a sharp knife, slice yams crosswise into ½-inch (1.25-centimeter) discs.

2. In a 4- or 5-quart (4- to 5-liter) slow cooker, combine yam slices, sea salt, cloves, coconut oil, and maple syrup with a wooden spoon to coat yams completely.

3. Pour orange juice over top.

4. Cover and cook on low for 2½ to 3 hours or until yams are tender.

5. Using a strainer, separate cooked yams from remaining juices.

6. Pour remaining juices into a medium skillet, set over high heat, and cook, stirring constantly, for 3 or 4 minutes or until juices reduce and syrup forms. (Be careful not to burn syrup.) Remove from heat immediately.

7. To serve, drizzle syrup over yams and top with chopped pecans.

It's okay if you don't want to make the syrup reduction for this recipe. The yams will still be sweet and delicious served with a small spoonful of the cooking juices and topped with nuts.

Candied Yams

Glossary

allspice A spice named for its flavor echoes of other spices such as cinnamon, cloves, and nutmeg.

almond butter A thick paste made from ground almonds.

almond flour Blanched almonds, ground to a flourlike consistency; also known as *almond meal*.

almond milk A cream-colored liquid made from soaking ground almonds.

artichoke heart The center of the artichoke flower, often sold canned or frozen.

arugula A spicy-peppery green that has a sharp, distinctive flavor.

baking powder A dry ingredient used to increase volume and lighten or leaven baked goods.

balsamic vinegar A heavy, dark, sweet vinegar produced primarily in Italy from a specific type of grape and aged in wood barrels.

basil A flavorful, almost sweet, resinous herb delicious with tomatoes and used in many Italian- and Mediterranean-style dishes.

bay leaf The fragrant leaf from the bay laurel tree, used to season dishes.

bok choy A member of the cabbage family with thick stems, crisp texture, and fresh flavor perfect for stir-frying.

braise To cook with the introduction of a liquid, usually over a period of time.

brine A highly salted, often seasoned liquid used to flavor and preserve foods. Also to soak or preserve a food by submerging it in brine.

broil To cook in a dry oven under the overhead high-heat element.

broth *See stock.*

brown To cook in a skillet, turning, until the food's surface is seared and brown in color, to lock in the juices.

butternut squash A soft orange winter squash with a sweet flavor and thin rind.

caramelize To cook vegetables or meat in butter or oil over low heat until they soften, sweeten, and develop a caramel color. Also to cook sugar over low heat until it develops a sweet caramel flavor.

caraway A spicy seed used for bread, pork, cheese, and cabbage dishes. It's known to reduce stomach upset.

cardamom An intense, sweet-smelling spice used in baking and coffee and common in Indian cooking.

carob The flesh of tropical tree pods that's dried, baked, and powdered for use in baking. The flavor is similar to chocolate.

cayenne A fiery spice made from hot chile peppers, especially the slender, red, very hot cayenne.

celery root The bulbous root of a celery plant; also known as *celeriac*.

chanterelle An orange or yellow mushroom with a fringed top and prominent gills.

cheesecloth A white cotton fabric with a loose weave used to make herb sachets.

chia seed A tiny black, brown, or white seed that absorbs liquid and forms a gel-like consistency.

chile (or chili) A term for a number of hot peppers, ranging from the relatively mild ancho to the blisteringly hot habanero.

chile oil A vegetable or olive oil infused with hot red chile peppers.

chili powder A warm, rich seasoning blend that includes chile pepper, cumin, garlic, and oregano.

Chinese five-spice powder A pungent mixture of cinnamon, cloves, fennel seed, anise, and Szechuan peppercorns.

chipotle powder A powder made from ground smoked jalapeños.

chive An herb that grows in bunches of long leaves and offers a light onion flavor.

chop To cut into pieces, usually qualified such as "*coarsely chopped*" or with a size measurement such as "chopped into $1/2$-inch (1.25cm) pieces." "Finely chopped" is much closer to mince.

chorizo A spicy hard or soft pork sausage, common in Portugal and Spain.

cider vinegar A vinegar produced from apple cider, popular in North America.

cilantro A member of the parsley family often used in Mexican dishes. The seed is called *coriander* in North America; elsewhere, the plant is called *coriander*.

cinnamon A rich, aromatic spice commonly used in baking or desserts.

clove A sweet, strong, almost wintergreen-flavor spice used in baking.

coconut aminos A tamari-like condiment made from coconut sap and salt.

coconut flour A flour made from powdered coconut flesh.

coconut oil The oil extracted from coconut flesh.

collard greens A leafy green with a thick white stalk, from the same family as cabbage and broccoli.

coriander A rich, warm, spicy seed used in all types of recipes.

Cornish hen A small broiler chicken.

crimini mushroom A brown, richly flavored mushroom. The larger, fully grown version is the portobello.

cumin A fiery, smoky-tasting spice most often used ground in Middle Eastern and Indian dishes.

curry Rich, spicy, Indian-style sauces and the dishes prepared with them. Curry powder, a blend of rich and flavorful spices such as hot pepper, nutmeg, cumin, cinnamon, pepper, and turmeric, is the base seasoning.

deglaze To scrape up bits of meat and seasonings left in a pan after cooking, usually by adding a liquid such as wine or broth, to create a flavorful stock.

devein To remove the dark vein from the back of a large shrimp with a sharp knife.

dice To cut into small cubes about $1/4$-inch (6.5mm) square.

dill An herb perfect for eggs, salmon, cheese dishes, and vegetables.

dolma A dish made of highly seasoned vegetables, rice, or ground meat wrapped in grape leaves.

extra-virgin olive oil *See olive oil.*

fennel In seed form, a fragrant, licorice-tasting herb. The bulb has a mild flavor and a celery-like crunch.

fig A sweet purple fruit with small edible seeds.

flaxseed A small, glossy brown seed from the flax plant.

flour Grains ground into a meal. Wheat is the most common flour, but oats, rye, buckwheat, soybeans, chickpeas, and others are also used.

fold To combine a dense and a light mixture with a gentle move from the middle of the bowl outward to preserve the mixture's airy nature.

frittata An egg dish that's cooked slowly, without stirring, in a skillet and then either flipped or finished under the broiler.

galangal root A Vietnamese root vegetable from the same family as ginger.

garam masala A blend of spices similar to curry.

ginger A flavorful root available fresh or dried and ground that adds a pungent, sweet, and spicy quality to a dish.

goji berry A red or pink Chinese dried berry with a high nutritional value.

granulated garlic A powdered form of garlic, often coarser than a fine powder and with no salt added.

ham hock A cut of pork found between the leg and foot, often smoked.

harissa A hot paste made of chile peppers.

herbes de Provence A seasoning mix of basil, fennel, marjoram, rosemary, sage, and thyme, common in the south of France.

hot pepper sauce A spicy, vinegar-based sauce made with hot chile peppers.

hummus A thick, Middle Eastern spread typically made of puréed chickpeas, lemon juice, olive oil, garlic, and often tahini.

immersion blender A handheld blender that can be submersed directly in a soup or stew to purée ingredients.

infusion A liquid in which flavorful ingredients such as herbs have been steeped to extract their flavor into the liquid.

Italian seasoning A blend of dried herbs, including basil, oregano, rosemary, and thyme.

jicama A large, round vegetable that's juicy, crunchy, and sweet.

kalamata olive Traditionally from Greece, a medium-small, long black olive with a rich, smoky flavor.

kale A dark, leafy green with a fibrous stalk.

kielbasa A ring-shaped smoked sausage popular in Poland and North America.

kosher salt A coarse-grained salt made without additives or iodine.

leek An onionlike vegetable with a mild flavor, white root, and dark green stem.

lemongrass A traditional Asian herb used for flavoring, cleaning, or in herbal teas.

marjoram A sweet herb similar to oregano popular in Greek, Spanish, and Italian dishes.

mince To cut into very small pieces, smaller than diced, about $1/8$ inch (3.18mm) or smaller.

mung bean sprouts Large, fresh sprouts from a mung bean.

mustard greens Dark, bitter, spicy greens from the mustard plant.

nori A thin sheet of edible seaweed often used to wrap sushi or as a garnish for soup.

nutmeg A sweet, fragrant, musky spice used primarily in baking.

olive oil A fragrant liquid produced by crushing or pressing olives. Extra-virgin olive oil, the most flavorful and highest quality, is produced from the olives' first pressing; oil is also produced from later pressings.

oregano A fragrant, slightly astringent herb used often in Greek, Spanish, and Italian dishes.

oxidation The gradual browning of a fruit or vegetable from exposure to air. Minimize oxidation by rubbing cut surfaces with lemon juice.

oxtail A cut of beef from the tail of cattle.

pancetta Cured and unsmoked pork belly.

paprika A rich, red, warm, earthy spice that lends a rich red color to many dishes.

parchment paper A brown, nonstick paper used in baking that does not contain wax.

parsley A fresh-tasting green leafy herb, often used as a garnish.

parsnip A long, cream-colored vegetable similar to a carrot.

pearl onion A small white onion, usually about 1 inch (2.5cm) in diameter.

pinch An unscientific measurement for the amount of an ingredient you can hold between your finger and thumb.

portobello mushroom A large, brown, chewy, flavorful mushroom.

purée To reduce a food to a thick, creamy texture, typically using a blender or food processor.

ragout A French term for a stew served as the primary meal, often accompanied by rice or pasta.

raw honey Unprocessed honey.

reduce To boil or simmer a broth or sauce to remove some of the water content and yield a more concentrated flavor.

rosemary A pungent, sweet herb used with chicken, pork, fish, and especially lamb.

saffron A yellow, flavorful spice made from the stamens of crocus flowers.

sage An herb with a slightly musty, fruity, lemon-rind scent and sunny flavor.

sauté To pan-cook over lower heat than what's used for frying.

savory A popular herb with a fresh, woody taste.

scallion A small, undeveloped onion with a white bulb end and hollow green stalks.

sea salt Salt made from evaporated seawater.

sear To quickly brown the exterior of a food, especially meat, over high heat.

sesame oil An oil made from pressing sesame seeds. It's tasteless if clear and aromatic and flavorful if brown.

shallot A member of the onion family that grows in a bulb somewhat like garlic but has a milder onion flavor.

shiitake mushroom A large, dark brown mushroom with a hearty, meaty flavor.

simmer To boil gently so the liquid barely bubbles.

skim To remove fat or other material from the top of liquid.

spaghetti squash A yellow winter squash with a mild flavor and stringy, golden-colored flesh.

star anise A star-shaped, woody spice with a licorice flavor.

stock A flavorful broth made by cooking meats and/or vegetables with seasonings until the liquid absorbs these flavors. The stock is strained, and the solids are discarded. Stock can be eaten alone or used as a base for soups, stews, etc.

straw mushroom A small Asian mushroom.

sunchoke The root of a particular species of sunflower; also known as a *Jerusalem artichoke*.

sweet potato A starchy, sweet, cream-colored root vegetable, similar to a yam.

Swiss chard A tender leafy green, often with bright yellow, pink, orange, red, or white stalks.

tahini A paste made from sesame seeds used to flavor many Middle Eastern dishes.

tamarind A sweet, pungent, flavorful fruit used in Indian-style sauces and curries.

tarragon A sweet, rich-smelling herb perfect with vegetables, seafood, chicken, and pork.

Thai chile A small, hot, red pepper popular in Thai cuisine; also known as *bird's-eye chile*.

thyme A minty, zesty herb.

turmeric A spicy, pungent yellow root. It's the source of the yellow color in many mustards.

turnip A mild root vegetable with a white root end and purple or red top.

vinegar An acidic liquid often made from fermented grapes, apples, or rice and used as a dressing and seasoning.

white mushroom A button mushroom with an earthy smell and appealing soft crunch.

yam A starchy, sweet, root vegetable similar to a sweet potato with an orange, pink, or purple color.

zest Small slivers of peel, usually from citrus fruit.

Index

U–V

W–X–Y–Z